when your child *has...* Autism

✓ Get the Right Diagnosis

✓ Understand Treatment Options

✓ Help Your Child Succeed

Adelle Jameson Tilton
Series Editor: Vincent Iannelli, MD

adamsmedia
Avon, Massachusetts

Published by
Adams Media, a division of F+W Media, Inc.
57 Littlefield Street, Avon, MA 02322. U.S.A.
www.adamsmedia.com

Contains material adapted and abridged from *The Everything® Parent's Guide
to Children with Autism* by Adelle Jameson Tilton, copyright © 2006 by F+W
Publications, Inc, ISBN 10: 1-59337-041-5, ISBN 13: 978-1-59337-041-1.

ISBN 13: 978-1-59869-676-9
ISBN 10: 1-59869-676-9
Printed in the United States of America.
J I H G F E D C B A

Library of Congress Cataloging-in-Publication Data
is available from the publisher.

This publication is designed to provide accurate and authoritative information
with regard to the subject matter covered. It is sold with the understanding that
the publisher is not engaged in rendering legal, accounting, or other professional advice. If legal advice or other expert assistance is required, the services of
a competent professional person should be sought.

—From a *Declaration of Principles* jointly adopted by a Committee of the
American Bar Association and a Committee of Publishers and Associations

Many of the designations used by manufacturers and sellers to distinguish their
product are claimed as trademarks. Where those designations appear in this book
and Adams Media was aware of a trademark claim, the designations have been
printed with initial capital letters.

When Your Child Has . . . Autism is intended as a reference volume only, not as a
medical manual. In light of the complex, individual, and specific nature of health
problems, this book is not intended to replace professional medical advice. The
ideas, procedures, and suggestions in this book are intended to supplement, not
replace, the advice of a trained medical professional. Consult your physician
before adopting the suggestions in this book, as well as about any condition that
may require diagnosis or medical attention. The author and publisher disclaim
any liability arising directly or indirectly from the use of this book.

*This book is available at quantity discounts for bulk purchases.
For information, please call 1-800-289-0963.*

Contents

Chapter 3 *Behaviors Associated with ASD and Your Child...41*

Chapter 4: *Communication—Challenges and Breakthroughs...69*

Chapter 5: *Putting Together an Early Intervention Team...85*

Introduction

With worldwide diagnoses of autism increasing dramatically over the past decade, you are one of many parents looking for answers about this and other disorders on the autism disorder spectrum.

You may be one of the parents who saw your beautiful baby begin talking, expressing his happiness and interest in the world around him, only to see him begin to regress and retreat into a world that seemed all his own. After watching this transformation in your child, it may come as a relief to finally have a diagnosis of autism so you can begin to help your child—by finding ways to help him communicate and interact with those around him.

You are already taking the first steps toward helping your child with autism to become the best person he can be. By reading this book, you are seeking out information about autism, wanting to know more about its symptoms, potential causes, treatment options, and available resources for your family. The study of autism can raise more questions than answers, but the more information you are armed with, the better prepared you are to be an advocate for your child.

With *When Your Child Has . . . Autism,* you can learn more about nonverbal communication and about the conceptual thinking that children with autism struggle with. You will learn about tools that can help you to improve your nonverbal communication skills, teach your child to use communication systems like communication boards and picture communication systems, and interpret your child's behaviors (whether meltdowns or flapping), all of which will help you to draw your child out from his private world and encourage him to explore and discover his own interests.

As a parent, the journey of autism isn't likely one you anticipated for your child. But it is one that you can travel with your child, experiencing small triumphs, remarkable successes, and a greater appreciation for your family's strength and the beautiful child you've brought into the world.

Chapter 1

The World of Autism

Ten Things You Will Learn in This Chapter

- What differentiates autism spectrum disorders
- The signs and symptoms of classical autism
- How to respond to echolalia
- The details of the Theory of Mind
- What exactly "conceptual thinking" means
- About the history and diagnosis of Asperger's syndrome
- Which of the autism spectrum disorders have been confirmed as genetic
- What defines high-functioning autism
- The differences between autism and Asperger's syndrome
- Possible causes of autism

What Are Autism Spectrum Disorders?

Learning about autism spectrum disorders is a bit like learning an unfamiliar language. It is a new world, and the customs and behaviors may seem foreign. From the moment a physician gives the diagnosis, everything changes. In all likelihood, as a mom or dad, this will not be the parenting experience you had hoped for. There are pitfalls and disappointments along the way. However, the good news is that this world can be navigated successfully, and it can be the beginning of something different, full of adventure and accomplishment.

Often referred to as ASD, autism spectrum disorder is a broad classification of conditions sharing similar objective symptoms. Objective symptoms are those that can be observed by someone other than the patient, whereas subjective symptoms are those that only the patient experiences. For example, in the case of influenza, an objective symptom might be a fever or a rash; a subjective symptom might be fatigue or pain.

Many times ASD is referred to as PDD (pervasive developmental disorder). Historically, ASD has been the more commonly used term in Europe and has recently been accepted as the proper term in the United States as well. This differs from PDD-NOS, which will be discussed in more detail later in this chapter. All of the various conditions within the spectrum are labeled, and there are differences in how the various conditions manifest themselves.

Classical Autism

Autism is the most commonly known of the spectrum disorders. First written about in the 1940s by Dr. Leo Kanner, a psychiatrist at Johns Hopkins University, autism was rarely seen by physicians. Characterized primarily by communication and socialization difficulties, classical autism is a very isolating and frustrating condition.

DID YOU KNOW?

The word *autism* originates from the Greek word *autos*, meaning "self." This disorder was named *autism* because it was believed to be an excessive preoccupation with oneself, originating from a mother who would not love her child. This theory has been proved false, and autism is now recognized as a medical disorder.

Classical autism is part of the ASD, or PDD, category. It is the best known of the pervasive development disorders, and it is one of the largest classifications within ASD as well, rivaled only by PDD-NOS (pervasive development disorder "not otherwise specified"). ASD is a syndrome. A syndrome is a group of symptoms that indicate a condition. Syndromes, by their very nature, have many characteristics, and each patient will display or not display those symptoms in very different ways. As such, each case of autism can be different.

The Signs and Symptoms of Autism

Autism has a set of signs and symptoms that can appear differently in each child, and parents must remember that what is considered autistic in one child may not appear in another child who is also considered autistic. This is part of the time-consuming nature of the diagnosis of autism. Without a definitive lab test such as blood work, diagnosis is a process of defining and understanding the symptoms as displayed. As a rule, children with autism exhibit the following signs and symptoms that characterize all autism spectrum disorders to a great degree.

- Expressive and receptive communication and social deficits
- Insistence on routine and resistance to change
- Appearing to be "off in their own little world"
- Resistance to physical closeness such as hugging
- Attachment to "odd" toys such as kitchen utensils
- Parallel play (playing beside other children rather than interactively with them) and lack of imaginative play
- Sudden and apparently unexplainable anger and tantrums
- Repetitive behaviors and obsessive-compulsive disorder
- Splinter skills (excelling in a particular skill that is above the apparent IQ level)
- Appearing to have sensory overload in normal environments

The Struggle with Communication

There is a marked reduction in verbal communication, or a child may have no speech at all. Echolalia is a speech pattern seen in autism spectrum disorders in which a child echoes back the words spoken to him or her. It is an attempt to understand language. For example, instead of responding to a question with an answer, the question is repeated back.

Children with autism also have difficulties with nonverbal communication skills. It is problematic for a child with autism to understand, use, and interpret subtle nonverbal language cues, such as facial expression or tone of voice, and translate those into meaningful language.

The difficulty with communication often accentuates the other deficits in autism. Frustration is a common problem with a child unable to communicate his most basic needs, and the result of frustration is often anger. A child will either struggle to communicate or withdraw even further if he is unable to convey thoughts and feelings to others.

The Problem with Conceptual Thinking

Children with autism also struggle in a profound way with conceptual ideas and thought patterns. For example, a child with autism may associate leaving the house with putting on a coat. Now imagine that same child was outside without a coat on and the temperature dropped dramatically, and it began to snow. Although the child might have a coat with her, even in her hands, she will not put on the coat. Why not? She associates the coat with leaving the house, not with a solution to cold weather, and the concept of using the coat for protection is nonexistent.

Because of the difficulty the child has in understanding concepts, he or she becomes limited in many ways. The child does not recognize that other people have their own thoughts, feelings, attitudes, and beliefs, and the child becomes even more isolated. Much of the maturing process for children is based on conceptual thinking, and the inability to think conceptually adds to the communication difficulties of a child with autism.

The Theory of Mind (TOM)

At some point in a child's development, he becomes aware that he is an individual. More importantly, he realizes that other people are individuals as well. Unfortunately, this moment never comes for children with autism. People with autism are unable to understand that every individual has her own thoughts and perspectives on the world. It is part of the self-involvement typical of ASD. It causes social problems and communication difficulties, and she can come across as cold and unfeeling.

DOES THIS SOUND LIKE YOUR CHILD?

People with autism experience all of the same emotions that others do. The difficulty comes from their inability to recognize those emotions in others and to express empathy for those emotions. Do not think if your child does not display feelings that she doesn't have them. She does.

Theory of mind (TOM) is the ability to recognize that other people have their own thoughts and feelings. If the theory of mind is disrupted, it is not a sign of poor intellect or mental retardation. It seems to be related to language and social function; feelings are generally communicated through language and subtle social clues (such as facial expression and body language), and these are the primary areas that are deficient in autism and its related disorders.

Anger and Aggression

Although not all children with autism display aggression, it is a very common symptom, and temper outbursts and outright tantrums are common. These can range from a brief explosion to a full-fledged meltdown. Children with autism may also strike out through hitting and/or biting as well as by destroying objects and possessions.

A child with autism throwing a temper tantrum is not a child acting "spoiled" or "bratty." Unfortunately, parents of children with ASD hear these terms quite often. These behaviors are a symptom of a disorder, not a result of poor parenting skills.

PDD-NOS—What Do Those Letters Mean?

PDD, as mentioned previously, stands for "pervasive developmental disorder." NOS means "not otherwise specified." In real-life terms, this means that the physicians know that the child's disorder is within the pervasive development category or on the autism spectrum, but it does not neatly fit into any particular category. As

such, it is classified as a PDD that has no further speci-
fication—it isn't quite autism, isn't quite Asperger's, and
isn't quite CDD (childhood disintegrative disorder), or
any other PDD.

A BETTER PARENTING PRACTICE

If your child has been diagnosed with PDD, ask the
physician why this diagnosis was given rather than
autism or Asperger's syndrome. A PDD diagnosis
may stand between your child and benefits she is
entitled to.

PDD-NOS has essentially the same set of signs and
symptoms that autism does, but the severity of the
symptoms is not as extreme as that found in autism.
A child who has PDD-NOS may initiate speech, using
language that is appropriate to the context of the social
situation. There will be deficits compared to the milestones of normal childhood development; however,
they will not be as blatant as a child who has autism.
Echolalia is heard less often and auditory processing
skills are more advanced.

Social skills in a PDD-NOS child are also less of a
challenge. These children are able to interact to varying
degrees with parents, siblings, other adults, and children. Imaginative play may still be limited but interactive play is somewhat more common than it is with a
child who is autistic.

Asperger's Syndrome

Dr. Hans Asperger first documented Asperger's syndrome at the same time Dr. Kanner was writing about autism. Both physicians were unaware of the other's work, as open communication between German and American scientists was not possible during World War II. The two physicians, however, arrived at the same conclusion at a time when ASD had not yet been officially identified. European physicians diagnosed Asperger's syndrome, and American physicians diagnosed Kanner's syndrome, which was the name initially given to autism.

It was not until the early 1980s that Asperger's was brought into American diagnostic procedures, and it was a full decade later that Dr. Asperger's original paper on the topic was translated into English. It was during the early 1990s that Asperger's syndrome was placed on the autism spectrum and became a disorder independent of other spectrum disorders. Several signs distinguish Asperger's syndrome from other disorders on the spectrum:

- Essentially normal speech development with phrases used by age three
- Essentially normal cognitive development
- Essentially normal development in self-help and curiosity about the world
- Gross motor skills are often delayed and clumsiness is common

- Eye contact, facial expression, body language inappropriate to the social situation
- Difficulty establishing and maintaining peer relationships
- Difficulty expressing emotions and relating to others with those emotions
- Intense and persistent association with particular subjects, objects, or topics
- Repetitive mannerisms such as flapping
- Insistence on routine

Although the symptoms of Asperger's syndrome seem very similar to that of autism, the normal development of speech and motor skill difficulties distinguish this disorder. Keeping in mind there are varying degrees of severity in Asperger's, it becomes easier to understand why diagnosis of this particular form of a high-functioning ASD may be delayed for many years. There are adults who are just now receiving the diagnosis of Asperger's, having been thought of as odd or eccentric for decades.

The Subtle Cues of Communication

The most obvious symptom in Asperger's syndrome is the socialization impairment. So much of our society's communication is based on unspoken cues, such as hand gestures, body language, eye movement, and even the pauses in conversation. All of those convey emotions and messages that may be subtle, but they are crucial to understanding the meaning of what a person is saying. For a person with Asperger's, those nonverbal cues are totally missed, as they live in a literal world where words have only literal meanings.

DID YOU KNOW?

It is common to hear people with Asperger's syndrome refer to themselves as "Aspies." This is not a derogatory term; however, it should be used only with someone who is close, such as a family member.

It is possible for people with Asperger's to learn social mannerisms by rote, but they do not generally understand the meaning behind them, and consequently, socialization suffers. Often people will misunderstand what a person with Asperger's is trying to say because of the literalness of the conversation. These misunderstandings can lead to hurt feelings and anger.

Asperger's and Autism

One challenge for parents is distinguishing Asperger's syndrome from autism in a very young child. If the parents have no other children, they may not have a frame of reference for comparison, or they might not realize how disordered the structure of the Asperger's social world is. In addition, if a child is very talkative and seems somewhat advanced in her interests, the parents may think the child is unusually gifted rather than narrowly and persistently focused on a subject, object, or topic.

It is important for the child to have an early diagnosis that is accurate so appropriate intervention can begin. Testing by qualified medical professionals can determine where a child falls on the autism spectrum and what treatments and therapies should be initiated. As with all disorders on the spectrum, early intervention offers the best hope for a promising future.

High-Functioning Autism

High-functioning autism (HFA) is a disorder on the autism spectrum that is often confused with Asperger's syndrome. It is, however, a distinct disorder. There is controversy about HFA because of the standard used to separate it from classical autism.

Statistically, many experts feel that approximately 75 percent of children with autism are mentally retarded. The technical standard for determining high-functioning autism and classical autism is the presence of mental retardation. In the past, a child with autism who was retarded was considered to have classical autism, and if retardation was not present, the disorder on the spectrum was high-functioning autism. If your child has a diagnosis of autism, do not assume he or she is retarded, as this may be the furthest thing from the truth. This is a very gray area and extremely difficult to determine for children on the autism spectrum.

The reason that this is a hotly debated issue is because of the difficulty of accurately measuring IQ in nonverbal children, as tests are constructed so that verbalization and the ability to conceptualize are mandatory. If a person is nonverbal and is unable to understand concepts, they will fail miserably at this method of determining intelligence. A score of seventy or below on an IQ test indicates a person is mentally retarded. However, a child with autism may not be measured accurately with the standardized IQ testing. Many physicians feel that children are inaccurately labeled as being retarded, which makes the line between classical autism and high-functioning autism harder to determine.

DOES THIS SOUND LIKE YOUR CHILD?

There are gender tendencies in autism spectrum disorders. Seventy-five percent of children with autism and PDD-NOS are boys. Asperger's syndrome affects boys at a ratio of 10 to 1 over girls. Fragile X and childhood disintegrative disorder are also more prevalent in boys. The only ASD to affect girls almost exclusively is Rett syndrome.

In everyday life, for parents, teachers, and most medical professionals, high-functioning autism is autism that is less debilitating than classical autism. If spectrum disorders could be viewed on a scale, high-functioning autism would fall between classical autism and PDD-NOS. As stated before, there is a fine line between HFA and Asperger's—the primary difference is in the motor skills. Although there are always exceptions, children with classical or high-functioning autism will not have the deficits in motor skills that a child with Asperger's displays.

Rett Syndrome and Other Spectrum Disorders

This spectrum disorder is unique, as it affects girls almost exclusively. Until recently, it was thought that a male fetus could not survive the disorder, and therefore all victims were female. Research now shows that although Rett syndrome is rare in boys, it should not be excluded as a diagnosis just because of gender. Rett syndrome is a genetically caused disorder.

A gene mutation causes Rett syndrome, and the degree of the mutation determines the severity of the condition. If a boy does have Rett syndrome, he will display the symptoms differently than a classic Rett syndrome girl, and therefore DNA testing is required to determine this disorder in boys. Rett syndrome is a rare condition, affecting only 1 in 100,000 children. The diagnosis of Rett syndrome is made by the observation of symptoms similar to autism. However, the differences between the two conditions become more apparent as the child ages, due to the dramatic regression exhibited in Rett syndrome. Indicators of Rett syndrome include:

- Frequent hand-wringing motion, which is unique to this disorder
- Major milestones as an infant achieved
- Loss of skills and abilities beginning at age two with increase in hand wringing
- Loss of the ability to walk
- Profound retardation
- Social skills decreasing with age

Girls with Rett syndrome are often misdiagnosed as being autistic when they are very young because of the similarities of symptoms. It is as the child ages, between the ages of five and ten, that the differences become apparent. The distinctive hand wringing is indicative of the disorder, and it interferes with normal motor functioning.

There are other lesser-known disorders on the autism spectrum such as childhood disintegrative disorder, fragile X syndrome, auditory processing disorder, hyperlexia, Williams syndrome, Prader-Willi syndrome, and Landau-Kleffner syndrome. A handful of disorders seem to fall among the better-known disorders. Most of these disorders are characterized by some of the same symptoms as other disorders on the spectrum, but they are less severe in their number and/or intensity. Other disorders are rare and seldom diagnosed in the face of other, more accepted diagnoses.

Implications of an ASD Diagnosis

Actually receiving the diagnosis of a disorder on the autism spectrum is often the most difficult step you, as a parent, will encounter. Virtually all children with autism show the symptoms and can be diagnosed between the ages of two and four. The most common age for children to display the behaviors and traits of autism is between fifteen and twenty months. Although some children are born with certain qualities that cause their parents to take note and observe them for unusual behavior, it is most common for a child to develop normally up to about sixteen months and then begin to regress, losing skills that had been mastered. It is common for children with ASD to have normal speech and behavior patterns for a child of fifteen to twenty months and then lose that behavior and speech, retreating into a world that they alone occupy.

However, the issue is not so much about at what age autism strikes as it is about getting an early diagnosis. A correct diagnosis for a child at a very young age means treatment and intervention at a very young age. Those interventions can make all the difference in a child's future. If a child receives therapy and treatments beginning at approximately age two or three, the long-term outlook is much better.

Although each child will display his particular type of ASD in a unique way, there are symptoms that form a consistent basis upon which to diagnose the disorder. The different degrees of these symptoms will determine the particular diagnosis of which disorder it is.

The three main categories that characterize ASD are social interaction, communication, and patterns of behavior, interests, and activity. Within these three categories are four criteria that are then used to determine if the diagnosis of an ASD is appropriate. At least one of the signs within each category along with a minimum of six signs from all of the categories must be met for a diagnosis of ASD.

DID YOU KNOW?

The *Diagnostic and Statistical Manual of Mental Disorders,* 4th edition, published by the American Psychiatric Association, is the manual used to diagnose autism spectrum disorders. In other words, whether a patient sees a physician in New York City or Cleveland, Ohio, the same standards are applied to diagnose a particular disorder.

Children with autism usually display the signs readily whereas pervasive developmental disorder, which is diagnosed with fewer than six signs, may be more elusive. The same symptoms exist but in a milder form. Sometimes parents need to seek out consultations with several experts to determine the exact diagnosis in less extreme cases.

Social Interaction

How a child interacts socially is the first of the three categories examined to ascertain whether an autism spectrum disorder is present. The physician will be involved, and it is likely a psychologist or psychiatrist may examine the child as well. Other experts will be consulted if needed. Doctors will look for

- Reduction or absence of eye contact, facial expressions, and/or body language
- Inability to form friendships within a peer group

- Unwillingness or inability to share enjoyment or accomplishments with others
- Inability to relate and share emotions on a social level

The impairment of social skills in a child with autism becomes obvious to a parent when a child is young. As a child matures, the interaction skills within the peer group isolate the child further, as he or she is unable to relate to other children and adults.

Communication

Communication is the second area experts analyze to determine if autism or a related condition is present. This exam involves a physician, speech therapist, and possibly other experts such as a psychologist or psychiatrist. The communication difficulties in an ASD child are typical to most of the conditions on the spectrum. These include

- Reduction, absence, or loss of expressive (spoken) language
- No attempt to replace language with another method of communication
- Inability to converse with another person even if speech is present
- Repetitive use of words, or echolalia (echoing words without meaning)
- Absence of imaginative play typical to a specific age group

Communication is imperative for a human being to function successfully. This impairment may be the most blatant and painful for parents to understand and cope with on a day-to-day basis. A child may have had language at a young age, perhaps saying "mommy" or "daddy" or identifying various objects within the house, and then lose those words completely.

DOES THIS SOUND LIKE YOUR CHILD?

The behaviors of autism may seem strange at first, but upon consideration, you will see that they reflect the child's effort to establish predictability and order in his or her world. A world with limited language, or no language at all, is out of control. A repetitive behavior can help the child gain some control.

A child may be suspected of being deaf because of the total lack of response to spoken language. It is common for the diagnostic trail to begin with a parent or grandparent asking for an auditory test because of the child's apparent lack of hearing. However, when the tests show that the child's hearing is normal, further testing will lead to the ASD diagnosis.

Patterns of Behavior, Interests, or Activity

The behaviors in a child with ASD are very distinctive and will be an indicator of where on the spectrum a child places. This exam involves a physician, possibly a pediatric neurologist, various therapists, and possibly experts in the mental health field. They will look for characteristics such as:

- Intense preoccupation with a particular activity
- Compulsive engagement in routines that serve no practical function
- Repetitive movements such as flapping, spinning, and/or body movements
- Intense preoccupation with parts of a whole—for example, the spinning tires on a bicycle rather than the entire bicycle

The behaviors of ASD are perhaps the best known of the signs and symptoms. Most children with autism appear perfectly normal to the bystander until certain behaviors such as flapping or spinning indicate that autism or a related condition is present. These behaviors are an early indicator as well, and they may be what prompt parents to seek a medical opinion.

Why the Increase in Incidence?
Over the past few years, there has been considerable debate regarding statistics that show an increase in the number of children diagnosed as autistic or on the spectrum. Has the number of children with autism increased, or has better diagnostic criteria resulted in the appearance of a higher incidence? This question has the autism community divided.

Autism was documented for the first time in the 1940s and it was theorized that "refrigerator mothers," those mothers who withheld love from their children, were causing autism. Because of that, it was labeled a psychiatric disorder and 50 percent of diagnosed children were institutionalized, forgotten by a society that never knew them in the first place.

Thirty years ago, the incidence of autism was between 1 and 4 per 10,000 children. It was a rare disorder, and few people had ever heard of it. In the recent past, though, the number of children with autism has exploded. It is difficult to find exact statistics on autism, but estimates by some research organizations show that it affects anywhere from 1 or 2 children per 500 to 1 per 100. The CDC reports a range of 2 to 6 per 1,000 children. The CDC reported that during the 2000–2001 school year, there were more than 15,000 children ages three to five years old and more than 78,000 children ages six to twenty-one years old in the United States with autism, as defined in the Individuals with Disabilities Education Act (IDEA). These estimated numbers are lower than the actual count, however, as students in private schools or homeschooling environments are not included.

The question remains whether the numbers are a true reflection of an increase of actual children with an ASD or if the procedures for diagnosis are simply more accurate now. Could it just be that it is recognized and properly labeled more often because our society has become better educated and more aware of autism and related conditions? Were children who had autism thirty years ago overlooked and therefore not treated? Many parents and researchers find themselves at odds over this point, and the children are in the middle of the debate.

DID YOU KNOW?

"Medicine for Autism Today," a neuro-immune dysfunction syndrome (NIDS) project, documented a study that illustrated the dramatic rise in the number of children with autism when they reported a 900 percent increase in cases of autism. Autism, according to this study, is growing faster than any other special-needs disorder in the world.

The unanswered question that essentially solves the debate pertains to adults. If autism has not increased in numbers and it is simply being diagnosed more carefully and accurately now, where are all of the adults with autism who were undiagnosed as children? Where are the children with autism who were born forty and fifty years ago?

A Look into Possible Causes

Nothing divides the autism community more deeply than a discussion of the potential causes of autism. Perfectly normal and rational adults will come together in meetings and benefits to raise awareness of autism issues and end up in bitter arguments as to what causes autism. The conflicts over vaccinations, genetics, disease processes, and allergies—to name a few—have driven deeply into the consciousness of parents with affected children. Many feel there is no one single cause but that a combination of triggers, combined in a unique way during this generation, has caused a cascade effect that has resulted in the condition we call autism and its related disorders.

There is no one proven cause of autism, but there are many suspected triggers. Aggressive research continues to be done in an effort to determine what the cause may be so that the most effective intervention can be put in place.

Neuro-Immune Dysfunction Syndrome (NIDS)/ Autoimmune Disease

Interestingly enough, when the number of autism spectrum disorders in the population began to increase, so did the incidences of autoimmune diseases and chronic fatigue syndrome (CFS), as well as attention deficit disorder (ADD/ADHD). It is common to find a family in which one parent suffers from CFS or another autoimmune disorder, an older child has ADD, and a younger child falls somewhere on the autism spectrum. It is as if something came into the environment of the house and attacked, affecting each member of the family differently based on his or her age.

The NIDS theory says that many, if not most, patients who suffer from a variety of autoimmune disorders, as well as autism, actually have a neuro-immune dysfunction. This causes chemical imbalances, which subsequently causes a restriction in the blood flow to the brain. In autism, the area of the brain affected would be the area controlling speech, language, socialization, and obsessive behaviors. The trigger that starts the disease process could be environmental, vaccine-related, or an illness.

If this theory holds true, then what is being dealt with is a new disease that has a great potential for treatment. This theory has not been proven, but physicians researching NIDS and the treatment of it are seeing relief of the symptoms of autism in their patients. Parents who have chosen these methods of treatment for their children are also seeing improvements they had only hoped for but never expected.

Vaccinations

One of the leading theories behind the cause of autism spectrum disorders is the increase in the number and kinds of vaccinations given to very young children. The leading suspect is the MMR (measles, mumps, and rubella) vaccination first given at approximately twelve to fifteen months of age. One study showed that upon biopsy of the lower gastrointestinal tract of children with autism, measles was found. This, of course, is not normal, and because many children with autism also have bowel diseases, it raised the question of what the connection may be. The study by Dr. Andrew Wakefield was later withdrawn though, and no link between the MMR vaccine and autism has been found.

A BETTER PARENTING PRACTICE

If you choose not to have your child immunized, upon entering school, you will need paperwork that states one of two reasons. You may claim a religious exemption or present a letter from your child's physician stating that he or she believes vaccinations are harmful to your child's health.

The research continues, and in the interim, many parents have decided against immunizations, despite the insistence of health organizations that there is no link between the MMR and autism. There are thousands of anecdotal stories about children who were perfectly normal until shortly after the first MMR immunization. These children spoke in phrases, interacted with people around them, and suddenly became nonverbal and nonresponsive within a few days of receiving the immunization.

Genetics

Many people believe that the cause of autism spectrum disorders will be found to have a genetic basis. Since many families who have one child with autism later have another one, it has led many to believe that autism "runs" in families. The only autism spectrum disorders that have been proven conclusively to be genetic are fragile X syndrome and Rett syndrome. Both of those disorders can be tested by blood work that looks directly at the chromosomes involved, and the genetic flaw can be identified.

The one hole in the theory that all autism spectrum disorders are genetic is that human genetics have not mutated very much over the past few thousand years, yet the incidence of autism is much higher now than at any time in history. Spontaneous gene mutations, which are especially more common in older parents, offer a newer genetic theory though.

Environmental Causes

Another theory that either stands alone or works in conjunction with the other theories is that environmental issues may have caused autism. The world is now inundated with pollution, food processing, and other toxic elements that were not present in past eras. It is conceivable that humanity has caused this syndrome by environmental abuse.

The most likely link with the environment intertwines with other theories, such as environmental factors combining with a vaccine and affecting DNA in a new way. At this time, like all theories, the truth is unknown.

Chapter 2

Coexisting Medical Conditions

Ten Things You Will Learn in This Chapter

- The difference between coprolalia and copropraxia
- How Obsessive-Compulsive Disorder and autism are related
- The behaviors associated with OCD and Tourette's syndrome
- Why routines are important
- The frequency of seizures in children with autism
- The effect of hearing loss combined with autism
- What hypersensitivity to sound feels like and the importance of sensory integration therapy
- Common indicators of visual problems
- How vision therapy can help
- Whether IQ tests for people with autism are accurate

The Truth about Tourette's Syndrome

It would seem that autism would be enough to deal with, but other medical conditions often accompany ASD. Some of these conditions are just those that happen to any child. *Comorbid conditions* are conditions that exist simultaneously within the same person. Other conditions occur with more frequency in an individual with autism and are thus known as associated disorders.

Often, parents of ASD-diagnosed children question whether or not their child may also have Tourette's syndrome (TS). TS is a neurological condition characterized by repeated and uncontrollable tics and/or vocalizations. This syndrome is diagnosed symptomatically, as there is no laboratory testing available to confirm the diagnosis. Signs include:

- Involuntary tics that are impossible to control for any extended period of time
- Tics that appear in repeated and consistent patterns
- Several motor and vocal tics that may or may not appear simultaneously
- Symptoms that occur for more than one year
- Symptoms that increase or decrease in severity over time
- Symptoms that manifest before the age of eighteen or twenty-one, depending on diagnostic criteria

TS is considered a spectrum disorder in itself, with different degrees of severity. Some people with TS have barely noticeable symptoms and others have problems with normal daily activities, as the rapid movements interfere to a great degree.

➤ DID YOU KNOW?

Tics are the involuntary movements of a portion of a person's body. These can occur anywhere in the body, but the face, neck, and shoulders are the most commonly seen locations for tics. Uncontrollable sounds made by a person are called vocal tics.

There is controversy and confusion as to whether the incidence of Tourette's is higher in children who have ASD. Some of the symptoms of Tourette's appear very much the same as the symptoms of autism. Some confusion may exist in the diagnosis of TS because TS and Obsessive-Compulsive Disorder (OCD) are linked, and OCD and ASD are linked. However, there does not appear to be a dramatically higher occurrence of TS in children with ASD.

Coprolalia and Copropraxia

One of the most recognizable symptoms of Tourette's syndrome is coprolalia—uncontrollable utterances of obscenities. However, this is seen less in children with autism due to the nonverbal issues. It is often combined with a gross motor tic called copropraxia, which is the use of obscene gestures.

Coprolalia only affects 30 percent of patients with TS, although it is the most commonly known symptom of the syndrome. Victims of this syndrome try desperately to mute the socially unacceptable words but, as with other types of tics, doing so only increases the compulsion. Ultimately, this effort increases, rather than decreases, the behavior.

Autism and Tourette's Syndrome

It is important to determine if a child has autism and Tourette's or if his or her tics may be a part of autism alone. Many children with autism have a series of tics that appear to be out of their control. With the repeated rhythm and compulsion to act out these tics, it is easy to confuse the two syndromes, but the compulsive aspects of autism are enough to cause this behavior.

If a child with an ASD has TS as well, it can be treated with various medications. However, medications should only be used if necessary, and a certain diagnosis is needed before such medications can be prescribed. A qualified physician can determine exactly what the diagnosis is and how to treat the disorder.

Obsessive-Compulsive Disorder Demystified

Obsessive-Compulsive Disorder (OCD) is an actual psychiatric disorder in and of itself, separate from autism. All disorders on the autism spectrum do show some degree of obsessive-compulsive behavior. ASD and OCD are closely linked. If a child has ASD, it is very likely she will deal with an element of OCD as well. OCD symptoms can be quite debilitating:

- Thoughts and/or images are recurring and persistent.
- Anxiety, sometimes severe, results from the thoughts and images.
- Thoughts and images experienced are not normal worries experienced by all people.
- Patients realize these thoughts are irrational but are unable to stop them.
- Behaviors such as counting, hand washing, or any number of activities are done repetitively.
- Behaviors are compulsive and produce anxiety if not performed.
- Compulsive behaviors are not linked in any rational way to the anxiety they are intended to reduce.
- Obsessions and compulsions interfere in a person's daily activities because of the amount of time they involve.

In a person with another condition, it is often difficult to separate out what might be OCD and what is part of the original problem. This is particularly true with an ASD. Autism by its very nature includes obsessions and compulsions as part of the matrix of symptoms. Children with an ASD will compulsively put objects in a line, insist that things are ordered in a certain way, and demand that a certain routine be followed, and they will become anxious and belligerent if these behaviors or routines are interrupted.

DOES THIS SOUND LIKE YOUR CHILD?

There are many theories as to why lining up objects is an almost universal symptom in autism, but it is an obsession and a compulsion. If the lines are disturbed, it is extremely frustrating to a child with autism. It may be an attempt on the part of the child to establish order during times of sensory overload.

If a child is diagnosed as having OCD and is not diagnosed on the autism spectrum, but the parents feel that there is a possibility of autism, it is important to seek a second opinion. If autism is present, even high-functioning autism, and early intervention is not provided, the possibilities of tremendous advancement at a young age may be lost. Do not hesitate to follow your own instincts regarding your child's health. A pediatric neurologist familiar with autism is a resource that should be considered.

Why Seizures Happen

Of all the conditions that can occur with autism, perhaps none is as frightening to parents as seizures. Parents feel out of control and fearful for their child. It may be more frightening because most seizures in children with autism do not begin until puberty, so the family has not gotten used to handling them. However, the condition is not as common as many parents fear; it is estimated that 25 to 30 percent of children with autism also have a seizure disorder. Most children on the autism spectrum make great strides during their teenage years, and negative anticipation is not warranted.

Since the seizures most commonly begin at puberty, and hormones become quite active at that time, researchers are looking for the connection between hormones and the chemicals within the brain. This could perhaps lead to testing that would predict which children might have seizures and to treatments that would prevent seizures from occurring.

Hearing and Auditory Response

A child with an ASD is not immune to the normal vision and hearing disorders that any other child may deal with. The problem for parents is recognizing when a problem exists.

Generally, hearing losses are discovered quickly in ASD children because of the suspicion of a child being deaf before an ASD is considered. It is common for parents, and especially grandparents, to question whether a child can hear due to the behavior of the child when a family member speaks to him or her. Normally, children turn their heads to acknowledge their name or to look in the direction of an interesting sound. Children with autism do not always respond to voices, and this may be the first thing you notice.

Hearing tests are very accurate, even on very young children. Audiologists will use special equipment to rule out a hearing loss. If there is a deficit in hearing, they will then determine what kind of deafness is occurring and how to treat it. If a child has a hearing loss, whether total or partial, it is important to intervene with the appropriate hearing aids, even if a child is totally non-verbal. Speech therapy is an important part of the intervention used for a child with ASD, and a child must hear properly to learn to integrate speech into her life. If she is not hearing sounds properly, it will be even more difficult for her to compensate for and possibly conquer the lack of speech.

A BETTER PARENTING PRACTICE

Sign language is the communication tool for the deaf. Although American Sign Language (ASL) is most commonly used, it is not the easiest for an ASD child to learn, as it is very conceptual. Exact Sign Language is more suitable for the way the autistic brain works.

There are even more problems if a deaf child is autistic, as the hearing impairment may mask the symptoms of autism, and the autism may not be recognized early in the child's life. This delays intervention and therapy that a child with autism so desperately needs.

Another common problem for children with ASD is being hypersensitive to sound. It is not unusual to see a child who has autism suddenly cover his or her ears in an effort to block out all sound. One theory on this is that people with autism do not discriminate sounds. In other words, they hear all sounds equally. As you sit here reading this book, you are most likely aware of sounds around you: traffic on the street, the hum of a heater or air conditioner, a radio, a dog barking in the distance, or any variety of the normal sounds of life. If this theory is correct, children with autism hear all of these sounds with equal intensity. It wouldn't take much of that to cause a sensory overload!

Whether it is not enough sound or too much sound, hearing is an issue for a person with an ASD. This sense is a vital part of functioning in the world, and a child needs to learn how to manage it. Appropriate therapy, especially sensory integration therapy, is vital to success in this area.

Vision Problems

Parents generally look out for vision problems by observing how their child watches television, colors pictures in a coloring book, or gauges distance while playing. A child with autism will do these things in the same manner as other children, so the unique visual problems of a child who has an ASD may be missed.

Identifying the Problem

Most children with autism have some kind of visual problem that results from being on the spectrum. Common indications for visual difficulties include:

- Lack of eye contact
- Staring at objects, especially spinning items such as wheels

- Momentary peripheral glances
- Side viewing
- Scanning objects quickly
- Difficulty maintaining visual contact with an object or person
- Crossed eyes
- Eye movement abnormalities

Vision problems are more typical in their occurrence with sensory disorder patients than in the normal population. Yet, when a child has autism, it is very easy for school staff, caregivers, and parents to attribute behaviors to autism when visual problems are the actual culprit. Combined with the problems a child with autism has in integrating visual input with other sensory input, this can lead to difficulties that are very hard to overcome. As an example, when there is difficulty integrating central vision with peripheral vision, processing is less efficient in the brain. This overlaps into other areas and can affect motor, cognitive, and speech skills.

Vision Therapy

Vision therapy is a specialized area of eye care. The specialists who practice in this field are known as developmental optometrists. These doctors are qualified to do vision exams and check for particular vision conditions. They can prescribe special lenses that will help with the integration of a child's vision and can prescribe therapies that will improve vision and sensory integration skills. These therapies are important to maximize the potential of a child's vision, reduce the likelihood of surgery and alert parents to any eye diseases that require an ophthalmologist.

DOES THIS SOUND LIKE YOUR CHILD?

One easy way for parents to determine if their child is having visual processing problems is to observe how she watches television. Does she press her face sideways to the screen and rotate her eyes around looking for a better angle? If so, an eye exam is in order.

Visual health is important, but just as important is visual processing. If an individual on the autism spectrum cannot process the information he or she receives through sight, the entire chain of sensory skills will not be in proper working order. The potential effects of poor visual processing can be multiple. Children can have attention span problems, an inability to recognize objects from different angles, and further delays in speech and sensory skills.

The visual abnormalities likely in children with autism can cause a total distortion in how they view the world and how they process that information. It can give a child the feeling that objects bounce or swim, jump unpredictably, are fragmented into tiny pieces, or are overly large. Poor visual processing will contribute to problems with fine motor skills, attention deficits, and a variety of social interaction issues. In order for a person to function as a whole, integrated human being, sensory integration must be functioning, and that begins with vision.

Other Physical Challenges

Some physical issues that accompany ASD are a part of the symptom matrix. Conditions such as encopresis, a complication of constipation characterized by leaky stool, and eczema are common in children with ASD. It is also common for these children to have abnormal reactions to sensations, such as the apparent inability to feel pain or an intolerance to heat or cold. Clumsiness or gross motor skill issues are common in Asperger's syndrome patients. Rett syndrome has its own set of physical issues that result in the loss of the ability to walk.

Any physical issues that may occur in the family are just as likely, or just as unlikely, to occur in the child with ASD. Migraines, allergies, ear infections, and any number of issues are not affected in either direction by autism. It may be harder for a parent to determine if a problem is present due to the communication difficulties and the different reaction to pain, but time and experience will teach parents how to cope with these problems.

Other Mental Challenges

ASD is characterized by deficits in mental functioning. The most difficult associated deficit is without a doubt mental retardation. Statistics vary widely on how many ASD children are also mentally retarded—the estimates range from 30 to 80 percent. Because of the difficulty in obtaining accurate IQ scores in children with autism, it is also difficult to determine if a child is mentally retarded. The standard for determining retardation is an IQ score of seventy or below.

With such a wide variance on the estimates of retardation occurring in ASD children, it is an area of great concern and great controversy. There is no "standard" retardation seen in ASD children, so the effect may be mild to moderate and even range to profound retardation in some individuals. When the level of retardation is mild, it is difficult to determine if it is truly a retardation issue or a problem with other symptoms of autism.

Retardation is difficult for parents to accept. Often, they emotionally cope with the diagnosis of autism easier than they do the diagnosis of mental retardation in their child. Be aware that many people with autism have extraordinary skills in a few areas. These are known as splinter skills and include such things as the ability to determine the day of the week of any given date in any given year. Splinter skills are remarkable feats of intelligence in very narrow areas. Having them, or not having them, does not indicate retardation one way or the other.

A variety of physicians and therapists should be involved if retardation is suspected. A pediatric neurologist is always the best physician for the primary care in autism, but a psychiatrist, a pediatrician, and a variety of therapists and psychologists should be involved as well. A team approach to a child with multiple deficits will provide for the best outcome.

There are no easy ways through this. Children on the autism spectrum have multiple problems of varying kinds. One child may have virtually no other physical or mental problems and another might have several. Most children fall in between and have a few problems along with the autism.

The most important thing a parent can remember is that not all of this will happen at once, and not all of it has to be solved at once. It is a matter of discovering the issues, determining the best course of action, and then beginning to walk the path. Your goal? Make your child with autism the best person he or she can be!

Chapter 3

Behaviors Associated with ASD and Your Child

Ten Things You Will Learn in This Chapter

- What the behaviors of autism look like
- Why lining up objects is important to a child with autism
- Why the autism community is divided on the medication debate
- Why children with autism insist on routine
- What flapping really means
- How to respond to aggression from your child
- Why elopement isn't always about marriage
- How an identification bracelet can help you
- That meltdowns are not the same as tantrums
- How to handle a very public meltdown

Obsessive-Compulsive Behaviors

The behaviors of autism are a hallmark symptom, after lack of speech. Behaviors that are out of the ordinary are the primary symptom in other spectrum disorders such as Asperger's syndrome. The behaviors shown in ASD are particular to the disorder, and although each child is unique in how he or she displays autism, certain behaviors are common. Some of these behaviors will interfere with daily life and others will not. Some can be controlled while others are just a part of the package that is your child.

Many behaviors fall into this category, and it is important to remember that although OCD may appear to be the same, it is not. However, the child with autism is obsessed with and compulsively engages in many behaviors, such as the following:

- Lining up objects, such as trains, blocks, cars, or DVD cases
- Opening or closing doors on cupboards, closets, or doors to the outside
- Spinning in circles or walking in a circle
- Hand or arm flapping
- Rocking the body back and forth
- Counting objects repeatedly for no apparent reason
- Hiding or hoarding objects
- Preoccupation with objects being placed in a chosen location

- Making gestures and facial movements that resemble Tourette's syndrome
- Narrow selection of food often based on color or shape

These behaviors have two parts. The first part is the obsession; it is uncontrolled and unwanted thoughts. Because people with autism are either nonverbal or have limited verbal ability, it is difficult to determine if those thoughts are present, particularly in children. The second part manifests as compulsive behaviors; parents, teachers, and medical experts easily see this aspect.

Lines

Some believe that the creation of lines, and the act of lining up objects, is the effort of the person with autism to put a sense of order to what he perceives to be an out of control and disordered world. If the sensory overload that children with autism have is common, it is easy to understand in this context. Lines are orderly and creating those lines gives control.

It is believed that people with autism do not have the discriminatory ability to separate environmental input. In other words, when the television is on, the air conditioner is running, the dog is barking, and the phone is ringing at the neighbor's house, people with autism perceive the sounds as all being of equal weight. The same analogy can be applied to the other senses as well. Sensory overload is a common occurrence for children with autism. It could easily be deduced that this "equal opportunity stimuli" would apply to visual input as well.

A BETTER PARENTING PRACTICE

The only negative aspect to line creation is the pre-occupation and absorption that may result. If that is the case, divert your child's attention into other activities that do not threaten his ability to create his lines. Most of the time, this behavior of creating lines diminishes as a child matures.

Lines are the perfect solution if the visual part of the brain is on overload. A line is the shortest distance between two points and that makes it clean and uncluttered. Lines may not be a meaningless compulsive behavior but may be a way of coping with sensory overload through an order that is natural and easily understood.

Medications

Parents of children with autism are very divided on the use of medications, particularly for issues of behavior, as opposed to seizures or other medical conditions. The medication commonly used for the compulsive behaviors of autism is known as a selective serotonin reuptake inhibitor (SSRI).

SSRI medications used by patients with autism have been shown not only to reduce compulsive behaviors, but also to aid in other symptoms of autism. Most notably, eye contact improves, social interaction becomes easier, the narrow field of interests grows, and the isolation problems of many children with autism lessen. Tantrums and anger are also reduced with the use of SSRIs. The primary symptom of children with autism being withdrawn and preoccupied within their own world is also lessened, and the medication has a calming effect.

Side effects are generally few and include dry mouth, insomnia, and paradoxically impulsive behavior. These side effects are rare and can be avoided by starting with very small doses and working up to the ideal dose. These medications are not recommended for people who have seizures or heart problems, so a consultation with a physician well acquainted with the use of these medications is prudent. Studies of ten years and longer do not show any long-term problems resulting from the use of SSRIs.

Routine

One way that obsessive-compulsive behavior manifests in a child with autism is through the insistence of routine. A sudden change in the daily routine, or even a small aspect of that routine, can cause a perfectly good day to go downhill fast. Routine is part of autism, and although flexibility can be taught to a certain degree, the need for routine will never disappear completely. Children with autism depend on that routine to know what is going on, what is expected of them, and what they can expect from others.

DID YOU KNOW?

In the case of separated or divorced parents, a child may have behavioral problems with the noncustodial parent when that parent has the child for a long weekend. This can lead to questions about the ability of a parent to care for the child. In reality, it is the change in routine that is to blame.

If your child is sensitive to routine changes, minimizing the shock of the change is a wise idea. Sometimes sudden change cannot be avoided, so all a family can do is remember how upsetting those changes are to a child with autism. When an unexpected event causes a routine change, such as a snow day that has canceled school, provide your child with a good movie or a favorite toy that hasn't recently been played with to distract her as much as possible. For the most part you will have to ride it out; it is just one of those things that everyone will learn to adapt to, including your child.

Figuring Out "Flapping"

Flapping is a behavior that can be considered a form of compulsive activity. It is common in all spectrum disorders, but is particularly strong in autism. It appears around the time of other autism symptoms and is linked to either strong physical actions or emotional activity. Flapping is a rapid and repetitive hand and/or lower arm motion that resembles waving. It is often one of the first symptoms that parents notice, as it is an atypical behavior in children.

Expressing Excitement

When a child with autism becomes excited, it is common to see this excitement manifested as flapping. Many children will be watching a television program or movie and become so excited that the emotion has to spill out; flapping will be the result. Positive emotions such as excitement, joy, or utter delight are more commonly associated with flapping than negative emotions. Flapping can often herald a loss of control and should be watched and regarded as a signal. Most of the time flapping means nothing more than the emotion it is connected to, but if an emotion is getting too extreme, flapping will usually precede it.

There are times when a child who is irritated or upset will flap. Parents will see a different "character" to this kind of flapping and will learn to recognize that anger or aggression may be building. This is something that only experience can teach. Learning to correctly anticipate behaviors is part of the parenting of a child with autism. As the months and years go by, it becomes much easier to accurately do this, so learn to trust yourself, as no one knows your child as well as you do.

Flapping is also seen in children with autism during physical activity. Most children will pump their arms while running. Children with autism will quite often not reach this developmental milestone and will flap while they run. This is related to the activity and not to any particular emotion.

Other Repetitive Behaviors

Flapping isn't the only repetitive behavior that appears in autism. Autism also causes other behaviors that are unique to the disorder. Such actions as twirling, rocking, head banging, facial contortions, eye movements, and unusual voice patterns are also repetitive stereotypical behavioral patterns. These behaviors are different from tics and other repetitive motion disorders, so a diagnosis of autism cannot be based on the appearance of these behaviors alone.

Behaviors such as head banging and facial contortions disturb parents greatly. It is an out-of-control behavior that displays the undeniable fact that a child is disabled. Lack of speech can be covered up; deficits in learning abilities can be glossed over. It is impossible to ignore a physical action repeated endlessly with no meaning.

Treatment

Physicians have different views on the treatment of flapping and related behaviors. The vast majority feels that if the movement patterns do not respond to the medications a patient with autism is already on, no further treatment will be effective either. SSRIs, Ritalin, and Risperdal are medications often used on patients with autism. SSRIs are often the medications that can halt behaviors specific to autism.

The best way for parents to handle these behaviors is to ignore them. It is unknown why people with autism engage in these behaviors, but it seems to fulfill a need. Interrupting the behaviors will only cause agitation, which can develop into aggression and anger. It is tempting to want to stop these behaviors, but resisting the urge will be less stressful for both parents and child.

Anger and Aggression

Unfortunately, the behavior that is most commonly seen in autism is anger that is expressed through aggression, tantrums, and outbursts. Meltdowns are an extreme form of an anger display. Of all of the issues in autism, dealing with anger is probably the most difficult.

Anger is caused by frustration, and frustration is an emotion that is prevalent in children with autism. When communication is difficult or not possible, it is only natural to become frustrated. Consider how you would feel if you were trying to explain something important to someone who does not speak your language. As you attempt to convey your thoughts and they are not being understood, your frustration grows; you feel frustrated with the situation and with yourself. If you consider that feeling in a child, the only outlet available is anger, and that is particularly so if the child does not grasp proper social interaction.

Getting Aggressive

Aggression is often the first indication of anger. Children with autism are often aggressive toward other people. They can also become aggressive with pets, toys, and household items.

A BETTER PARENTING PRACTICE

The medication Risperdal is often used to control aggression and anger in children with autism. It is important that parents watch for excessive weight gain and facial tics while their child is on this medication. If these side effects are observed, discuss them with your physician right away.

Anyone and anything can be on the receiving end of the seemingly rude and thoughtless behaviors that occur as a child with autism strives to get his own way. Keeping in mind the frustration a child feels when he is unable to convey his needs and wants, it is easy to understand why he might turn to whatever method will work to have those needs met. Any child, even one who is successfully learning the social graces of our culture, will become pushier than normal when he has to struggle to satisfy his needs. But a child void of social skills will turn to whatever behavior is successful, and often that behavior is aggression.

Tantrums and Outbursts

It is also common for a child on the spectrum who doesn't get her own way to show anger as a form of retaliation, resulting in an outburst or tantrum. When the child is prevented from having what she wants at any given moment, it can result in her hitting or slapping someone without any warning. Parents, siblings, teachers, and caretakers are the usual targets of retaliation. For example if your child wants a particular toy, or to play with something that you have denied her, your child may strike out in anger by hitting or biting.

It isn't unusual for the family dog or cat to bear the brunt of a child's lashing out as well. She may also throw or break things, which only makes the situation worse, as the child then becomes distressed over the broken item. The child has difficulty gaining control over this repeating cycle. Tantrums and outbursts can end as quickly as they began or may take some time to wind down.

Responding to Aggression

When a child has an explosion of anger, parents have to think on their feet. This isn't a problem you can analyze and try to solve—you do need to reflect back on the issue that brought the anger about for the sake of prevention, but the tantrum or outburst you are seeing now has to be dealt with now. It is better to resolve the problem quickly, even if it means giving in to your child's tantrum. It is always unacceptable for a child or adult to strike another person for any reason, at any time. This is the lesson you must convey. The easiest way to teach this is by understanding the cause of the outburst.

If a child loses control over an unmet need that is important, or that an adult did not realize was an issue, the situation will only get more out of control if the child is punished. There is enough of a problem with communication without your child feeling that you are punishing him for his attempts to let you know what's on his mind.

Elopement—Your Escaping Child

Elopement is something almost all parents of children with autism have had experience with at one time or another. Elopement in this case is not a child running off to get married; it is a child with autism escaping from his home and wandering off alone. It makes for sleepless nights and jittery nerves. Take the time to view your house as your child would. How can you prevent elopement? Here are some suggestions.

- Put extra locks on all doors that open to the outside.
- Install a security system that monitors both entering and exiting.
- Install an alarm that hangs on doors for use away from home.
- Get a service animal (a dog is most useful for this problem).
- Establish a routine in which the child never leaves the house unsupervised.
- Inform trusted neighbors of the possibility of elopement.
- Notify the local police department of the potential problem.

There are other hints that can help your peace of mind at the same time you are protecting your child's safety. A large family can work in shifts so that someone always has an eye on a child with autism. This is particularly important for a child that is bound and determined to escape. If Mom can't cook dinner or even escape to the bathroom for a few minutes, stress levels will rise and tempers will get shorter. The entire family must work together to lessen the stress on everyone.

DID YOU KNOW?

If you have an identification bracelet made, be sure you purchase one with a secure fastener. It should be made of stainless steel and have enough links on it to grow with your child. Put it on your child's non dominant hand so it won't interfere with things she does.

One solution that will work for any person with autism, regardless of age or size, is a double-keyed dead bolt. This type of dead bolt requires a key on either side to lock or unlock it. If you choose this method, the most important thing is to develop a habit of carrying a key with you at all times!! Put a chain around your neck with the key and have a key well hidden near the door. If a fire should break out, having a double-lock dead bolt can turn a safe situation into a deadly trap.

Wearing an identification bracelet is one of the easiest, and most important, steps parents can take to protect their child. MedicAlert has an inexpensive annual program that can protect your child in case of an accident or separation from the family. If you have a bracelet engraved, include the child's name, address, telephone number, allergies, and a physician's telephone number. Above the child's name have printed "Nonverbal Autistic" or "Limited Verbal Autistic" so that people are immediately aware of the child's situation.

Special Considerations

If you live near any potentially dangerous place, such as near water or near a busy road, it is imperative you have a locking safety system even if your child is not prone to elopement. All it would take is one escape and a child with autism could easily drown. Children with autism have been known to walk right in front of a moving car as they lack the ability to understand danger.

It is also wise to contact the city government for the town in which you live. Special road signs (the bright yellow diamonds) can be placed on both ends of your street that send a warning to drivers. It is wise to request a sign that says either "Disabled child at play" or "Deaf child at play." The sign for deafness is the most efficient, as drivers will then be aware of a child that is unaware of them. A sign that says "Autistic child at play," although accurate, can be less than helpful due to the lack of knowledge among the general public regarding autism.

A BETTER PARENTING PRACTICE

Children with autism usually outgrow the elopement problem. There are children who never do leave elopement behind, but they are in the minority. It is unclear if they simply lose interest or if they realize the level of danger, but the important thing to remember is that this is probably not a life sentence.

One of the most frightening forms of elopement can occur in the car. Without the realization of danger, a child with autism may open a car door while the car is moving. Always have your child safety-belted and in a car seat if she is under sixty pounds.

Take your car to a mechanic or dealer to have the inside door handle removed on one side only. In the case of an accident or other emergency, it is important that the other side of the car can quickly be exited. Always have your child with autism seated next to the door without a handle. If you can't find anyone to remove the handle, remove it yourself with a wrench and hammer. The cost of the repair, if you wish to have it replaced, is insignificant compared to the tragedy of a child falling out of a moving car.

The Law

The laws provide for reasonable accommodation for a disabled person in rental housing. If you have a child who elopes, or escapes, it is your right to have locks installed on the inside of doorways that the child is unable to open. Consider slide bars placed out of reach for younger children, and request a keyed dead bolt if you've got an older child who elopes. One trick that works well with a slide bar is to put it slightly out of alignment; the door handle has to be lifted slightly and a younger child is unable to unlock it.

If you live in rental housing, you may also ask your landlord to install window locks if your child attempts to elope through windows. In a pinch, a sliding window frame can have a nail hammered into it that will prevent the window from being opened any further than desired. Other window styles will have ways to jury-rig them, and until a permanent fix can be implemented, don't hesitate to do what you need to do to prevent an escape.

The law provides for reasonable accommodation for disabilities. You can't demand remodeling that is frivolous, unreasonable, or abusive of the disability laws, but safety and security are reasonable expectations. Asking the landlord to fence the entire yard so your child can play outside is unreasonable; but if you live in a rental with inadequate locks or other safety concerns, the landlord must immediately address and correct these issues without penalty of eviction.

Autistic Meltdowns and Temper Tantrums

Perhaps the true initiation of parenting a child with autism is the baptism by fire of the meltdown. Dealing with meltdowns is a bit like dealing with a tornado: You have very little warning, and about all you can do is ride it out.

A temper tantrum is very straightforward. A child does not get his or her own way and, as grandma would say, "pitches a fit." This is not to discount the temper tantrum. They are not fun for anyone.

Tantrums have several qualities that distinguish them from meltdowns.

- A child having a tantrum will look occasionally to see if his or her behavior is getting a reaction.

- A child in the middle of a tantrum will take precautions to be sure they won't get hurt.
- A child who throws a tantrum will attempt to use the social situation to his or her benefit.
- When the situation is resolved, the tantrum will end as suddenly as it began.
- A tantrum will give you the feeling that the child is in control, although he would like you to think he is not.
- A tantrum is thrown to achieve a specific goal and once the goal is met, things return to normal.

A temper tantrum in a child who does not have autism is easier to handle. Parents simply ignore the behavior and refuse to give the child what he is demanding.

DID YOU KNOW?

If you feel like you are being manipulated by a tantrum, you are right. You are. A tantrum is nothing more than a power play by a person not mature enough to play a subtle game of internal politics. Hold your ground and remember who is in charge.

If the tantrum is straightforward, the meltdown is every known form of manipulation, anger, and loss of control that the child can muster up to demonstrate. The problem is that the loss of control soon overtakes the child. He needs you to recognize this behavior and rein him back in, as he is unable to do so. A child with autism in the middle of a meltdown desperately needs help to gain control.

- During a meltdown, a child with autism does not look, nor care, if those around him are reacting to his behavior.
- A child in the middle of a meltdown does not consider her own safety.
- A child in a meltdown has no interest or involvement in the social situation.
- Meltdowns will usually continue as though they are moving under their own power and wind down slowly.
- A meltdown conveys the feeling that no one is in control.
- A meltdown usually occurs because a specific want has not been permitted and after that point has been reached, nothing can satisfy the child until the situation is over.

Unlike tantrums, meltdowns can leave even experienced parents at their wit's end, unsure of what to do. When you think of a tantrum, the classic image of a child lying on the floor with kicking feet, swinging arms, and a lot of screaming is probably what comes to mind. This is not even close to a meltdown. A meltdown is best defined by saying it is a total loss of behavioral control. It is loud, risky at times, frustrating, and exhausting.

Meltdowns may be preceded by "silent seizures." This is not always the case, so don't panic, but observe your child after she begins experiencing meltdowns. Does the meltdown have a brief period before onset where your child "spaces out"? Does she seem like she had a few minutes of time when she was totally uninvolved with her environment? If you notice this trend, speak to your physician. This may be the only manifestation of a seizure that you will be aware of.

A BETTER PARENTING PRACTICE

When your child launches into a meltdown, remove him from any areas that could harm him or he could harm. Glass shelving and doors may become the target of an angry foot, and avoiding injury is the top priority during a meltdown.

Another cause of a meltdown can be other health issues. One example is a child who suffers from migraines. A migraine may hit a child suddenly, and the pain is so totally debilitating that his behavior may spiral downward quickly, resulting in a meltdown. Watch for telltale signs such as sensitivity to light, holding the head, and being unusually sensitive to sound. If a child has other health conditions, and having autism does not preclude this possibility, behavior will be affected.

How to Handle a Public Meltdown

Any parent who is raising a child with autism will tell you that meltdowns are most common in public locations. Stores, malls, fairs—anywhere with a lot of people, activity, and noise raises the odds of a meltdown.

It is common enough that many parents will do anything they can to avoid being in those environments with their child.

At the Store

A parent related the following story about her son, and any parent of a child with autism will laugh and cry at the same time; they all know what this is like:

"We went in for groceries and various items. It was a big shopping trip and I couldn't find a babysitter that day. I also couldn't put it off any longer. We did okay until we went by the home gardening section. A big, and I mean very big, lawn sprinkler was on display—a sprinkler that was a dead ringer for the tractor that my little boy loves, all bright green and yellow and just about the right size for him to sit on. At first he quietly asked 'tractor,' or, should I say, demanded it. I could see the look. I knew he had decided the tractor was coming home with us. And I knew it wasn't. His tone of voice raised and raised until you could hear the word *tractor* being screeched all over the store! We made our way to the checkout line, but by then, he was in complete meltdown. I am sure that they thought I was the meanest mom in the world for not buying my little boy a toy tractor. The meltdown continued into the parking lot and into the car; he was sweating, crying, screaming, and attempting to hit anything or anyone he could. He totally lost it. I was exhausted and so was he." She added, "I now make an extra effort to find a babysitter and have my radar up to scope out the aisles around us to avoid any more tractors."

This mom handled this situation well. She had shopping that had to be done; this wasn't an optional trip to the store. And once the meltdown was in full swing, she was almost done. It wouldn't have been convenient for her to leave the store and return later to redo an enormous shopping trip. She kept her cool, didn't give in, and didn't worry about the opinions of others while her son spun totally out of control.

The Reactions of Others

The little boy with, or in this case without, the tractor had a real advantage that day. His mother was not threatened or concerned about the opinions of others. It has been said that parents of kids with special needs develop thicker skins, and it must be true. But regardless of how thick-skinned you are, an insult to your child cuts, and cuts deeply.

Keep in mind that some people are receptive to learning and you may have a chance to educate someone about autism. There are also subtle clues you can use to notify people without saying a word that you have a child with some special needs. The tractor incident brought out a creative action by the mom mentioned previously. She said that she liberally used sign language, even signs her son didn't know, as a way to communicate to observers that there was an issue with her son.

DOES THIS SOUND LIKE YOUR CHILD?

If your child begins a meltdown by putting his hands over his ears or eyes, you can be sure he is experiencing sensory overload. He might even cover your mouth with his hand to prevent another sound. The best thing is to move him to a low-sensory environment; a dark, quiet, and cool place will help.

It is very common for people in environments such as the store with the tractor to stare and make comments that are very critical of a child in the middle of a meltdown. People will say things about you not controlling your child (or use unflattering words toward your child), and as much as you would like to throttle them in the heat of the moment, resist the urge. Excuse your child's behavior politely with the brief explanation of "he is disabled," and drop it. If a person persists in making comments and it is clear they are not interested in educating themselves, move yourself and your child to another location.

Calming Your Child

Although it sounds like a cliché, the best way to handle a meltdown in progress is to defuse it. Sometimes that is much easier said than done, but it comes down to one simple sentence: Choose your battles. How you choose them will depend on your personality and your child's personality.

When Your Child Understands

When a child understands and manipulates a meltdown to get her own way, you are dealing with an intelligent child who can stop the behavior if it is caught in time. Keep in mind that a child with autism, regardless of how well she understands that her meltdown is not wanted, will not be able to control it once it reaches a certain point. The goal is to not reach that point if your child is cognizant of her behavior.

1. Recognize the signs that a meltdown is impending.
2. There is a certain trigger before the meltdown—determine what the trigger is.
3. If the trigger is fairly insignificant, such as him wanting to hold the red ball in the store, decide if it is worth it. A red ball is a small price to pay for a quiet shopping trip.
4. If the trigger is something that is not possible to resolve, such as the one in the tractor story, try to distract your child by moving to another location in the store and finding a reasonable substitute that will divert her attention.
5. If you are in a restaurant and a meltdown is approaching, reach for a new or very special toy you have hidden in your purse. Something complex, like a handheld puzzle, can work well.
6. As you are working to distract your child, speak softly to him about his behavior and let him know

that it needs to stop. Don't dwell on what he can't have at that moment, but reiterate that he needs to slow down and stay in control. Stay calm so he has no idea you are panicking over the thought that he might lose it.

7. Persist in any calming techniques that work for your child. Some children will respond to a hug while others will not want to be touched; this is a matter of "whatever works."

You will not always be able to defuse a child bent on having a meltdown. If the cycle progresses and he reaches the point of no return, you have two options. You can decide to ride it out or you can leave the environment. Keeping in mind that this child understands that he entered into this situation of his own free will and that you asked him to stop, it is often more of a learning experience to ride it out. It is not the easiest thing to do, but the goal is to help your child acquire long-term acceptable behavior patterns.

Much of riding it out depends on where you are. Right in the middle of a wedding may not be the best location to try to work with behavior modification. Other people, and those in certain locations, do have the right to have an undisturbed environment. However, in the real world, the everyday world, your child has to learn to operate in society, and society has to learn to deal with children with autism. It is more prudent to leave an area if others are being disturbed unfairly or the situation could become dangerous.

When Your Child Does Not Understand

A child who does not understand what type of behavior is wanted or expected of her is more challenging to deal with when a meltdown is about to occur. Parents will have the same warnings that they have with a child who does understand, but there is less they can do to stop the cycle. It is important to remain calm. Your child is already on a sensory overload and if you are upset, you will only aggravate that. Keep your voice even, quiet, and calm no matter what happens.

The primary tool a parent has with a child in this position is distraction. It is useless to try to reason with a child who does not understand that what he is doing is unacceptable. Molding a child's behavior through distraction and positive reinforcement will be a much more effective tool to stop the current problem and prevent future ones as well.

Parents can keep items handy in a backpack or tote bag to distract their child when the meltdown begins. When it becomes apparent that the fuse is just about burned out and the explosion is about to begin, being able to pull "the rabbit out of the hat" is your best bet. Comforting toys, such as a favorite stuffed animal, are wise choices, as are toys that are so fascinating that they just can't be ignored.

Avoid Meltdowns Altogether

What is easier than handling a meltdown or defusing one? Avoiding it altogether. You may feel right now that you have little control over the tantrums and meltdowns, and it's true that you don't have total control of them. However, there are things you can do to minimize the frequency and severity of the outbursts.

Working with a child's behavior is always the first step a parent should take. If you can modify the behavior that is undesirable, your child will be happier and those around him will be as well. Don't ever think you are being cruel by working to alter unacceptable behaviors. You will be met with resistance; no one likes to change, least of all a child with autism. But at times, change is necessary, and when a child has a predilection to tantrums, the behavior must be changed.

Applied Behavioral Analysis (ABA)

ABA is one of the most widely used methods to treat children with autism. Dr. Ivar Lovaas, the founder of the Lovaas Institute, is the creator of ABA. His goal in working with children with autism has been to modify behaviors that are inappropriate and replace them with appropriate behaviors.

As Lovaas developed his theories of behavior in people, the foundation of his work centered on how people treated one another—was it environment or genetics that caused people to act a certain way? By a twist of fate, he began working with children with autism and observed that modifying behaviors was not the difficult part. The hard part was keeping those behaviors solidly in place after the behavior had been successfully changed.

Lovaas realized that the main difference in behaviors between children with and without autism was based on the way that children learn. Children who do not have autism are constantly learning. Even beyond school, every moment of every day is a learning experience for a child. Learning is a constant and dynamic process. However, a child with autism goes to school and for a prescribed number of hours each day, he learns things. When he returns home, the structured learning is over for the day and he retreats into his own world.

Continuing ABA Therapy

The key to modifying behavioral problems in a child with autism suddenly became obvious to Dr. Lovaas. A child could not come to the Institute, work on ABA, and then just return home after successful therapy was completed; the newly acquired behaviors broke down and everyone was back to square one. It may seem obvious now, but at the time, this was quite a breakthrough. Parents were taught how to continue the ABA therapy at home and permanent changes in behaviors were seen.

If behavioral issues have had a profound impact on your child's life, and subsequently your family's life, behavior modification might be appropriate to investigate. See Appendix B for resources to learn more about this technique. Meltdowns and tantrums, if your child is inclined to them, will not disappear entirely, but there is an excellent chance these outbursts can be reduced dramatically with training and therapy.

Chapter 4

Communication — Challenges and Breakthroughs

Ten Things You Will Learn in This Chapter

- Why communicating with a nonverbal child can be intimidating
- The importance of assuming your words are understood
- How concepts are embedded in everyday language
- The definition of receptive speech
- When a speech therapist can help
- How American Sign Language works
- What Exact English is
- How to create a picture communication system
- How a laminating machine can help you communicate with your child
- Why there's controversy behind facilitated communication

A Nonverbal Person

Communication is, without a doubt, the most serious impairment that a person on the autism spectrum experiences. When a person—particularly a child—is unable to communicate, it is very difficult to understand and meet his or her needs. A child learns security and safety through having her needs met, so the lack of communication means more than not hearing those wonderful and exciting first words. Communication is the underpinning of our psychological makeup.

Communicating with a nonverbal child intimidates many people. If a child understands language, even if he is unable to speak, it is hard enough to communicate with a child. If a child doesn't understand that language, communication between that child and others is very difficult and emotionally trying for the family. However, what most people don't realize is that they are already very proficient in communicating with a nonverbal person.

And You Thought It Was Baby Talk!

When parents bring home their newborn, they begin communicating nonverbally. All the little cooing and babbling sounds that come from perfectly rational adults are the beginnings of communication without words. Tunes hummed to baby are another form of communication. It is through the tone and the rhythm of the voice that messages are sent. Although a baby does not have the ability to understand the complex messages literally, she begins to learn about communication from these sounds and their cadence.

Parents learn as well how to understand nonverbal communication. Parents learn to recognize when their baby cries whether it is hunger, discomfort, pain, or any number of things that are being communicated. Those first cries, and the subsequent response by a parent, are the first forms of reciprocal communication.

If only communication stayed that simple. As a child matures, his needs include much more than just hunger or comfort. He needs to convey emotions, complex needs, and desires, and it is very difficult without language. To keep things in perspective, remember that you have already established communication with your child. Yes, it was at a very young age and, yes, it isn't a fully efficient language. But you have the basics and you know more about nonverbal communication than you realize.

Trust Yourself and Pull Out the Stops

Much of the success in communication is about trust. If you believe your child will not understand, can never understand, and doesn't want to understand, you will probably find that to be true. But if you believe she can understand much more than anyone realizes and you continue to communicate with that belief, you will find that her abilities will increase.

Never assume that your words and sentences are not understood. Your child's receptive language may not be at 100 percent, but something, somewhere, will get through and that is all you need to build on. Talk to your child as you would any child. Don't talk down to him, and don't talk over his head. Work at getting eye contact so he can see your facial expressions. Stand in front of him so he can see your body language, even if he appears to be totally oblivious to it. Consider your tone of voice and use every visual clue you can think of.

DID YOU KNOW?

Do you talk to your cat? Kitty comes into the kitchen meowing, and someone will pick up the cat food and ask the cat if he is hungry. No one expects to hear the cat answer, but communication has occurred. There are lessons here for the parent of a child with autism—body language, tone of voice, and visual cues effectively communicate a message.

As the light begins to dawn for your child, and she realizes language is a useful tool, she will begin to attempt to understand it. It is a long and hard road for both parent and child, without a doubt. As the foundation begins with very little, and seemingly unimportant, understanding of minor words, you will realize that more complex receptive language skills can and will develop.

Why Conceptual Images Are So Important

For people with normal speech development, it is very difficult to communicate without using concepts. Things are big or bigger, happy or joyous, under, over . . . the list is endless. The human mind is built on and works through the understanding of concepts. But for someone with autism, concepts are very difficult to deal with. Can effective communication happen without relying on the conceptual imagery everyone uses each day?

A Language of Concept

Language by its very nature is conceptual. We believe, because we have been taught and we have seen the result, that these words are truly representative of something. If you go into an ice cream shop and ask for a large cone, you have certain expectations that you believe the other person understands. Generally, people do understand, and if they don't, they may ask for additional information.

Concepts within language are an obstacle for children with autism. When a word is first learned, whether verbal or through another form of communication, the use of that word has a hard and fast rule: A dog is always a dog; a cat is always a cat. But red? That is very subjective. Ask someone to go buy you a red hat and you will learn how many shades of red there are. Concepts such as quiet, hungry, or tired are even harder to grasp. Only time and experience can teach these lessons. Speaking normally with your child and using visual clues will help the process along, but there is no definitive method to teach a concept.

Echolalia

As a child begins to learn speech, it is common to see what is known as echolalia in children with autism. Echolalia is the repeating of words without using those words with any meaning. For example, a child can have a shirt or toy held up to him and a parent might say, "Is this your shirt or your brother's?" The response may be "Brother's." This may not mean that your child has signed off on the property in question; he may simply be repeating the last word he heard. If you are in doubt, test by using the question again, but reversing the order of words. If he repeats a different word, you can be sure it is echolalia.

A BETTER PARENTING PRACTICE

When talking to your child, use universal signs to help him understand. Spread your arms to indicate "big." Mock shiver for "cold." Use clues for your child to help him link the word with the object or action. As linkages occur, language will begin to make sense and communication will be more effective.

Echolalia is also seen with a child who is involved in activity. The child may repeat words she has heard during the day or words that are common to her routine. "Everyone sit down," "it's lunchtime," or "here kitty, kitty" are examples of phrases that might be said without meaning. Echolalia is frustrating to parents because they can see that the mechanics of language, such as the voice, are working fine, yet there is no spontaneous speech. When your child engages in echolalia in response to a question, try to guide her to the correct answer and gently correct her. If she is playing alone and you hear repeated phrases and words, ignore it. It is not helpful to try to stop a behavior that is harmless; she is unaware this is an inappropriate social behavior.

Clarifying Receptive Speech

Receptive speech is the ability of the human mind to hear spoken language from another person and decipher it into a meaningful mental picture or thought pattern, which is understood and then used by the recipient. Speech is the vocal expression of language.

A Confusing World

When a person has a deficit in his receptive language skills, the entire world is a mystery. People with autism are often assumed to be like people with deafness. But the inability to relate to others shows the difference between the two conditions. People with deafness can't hear sound, but they can understand the language and all the conceptual images within the words and put those to use within their own minds. People with autism hear the words but they do not have the same understanding of their meaning.

DOES THIS SOUND LIKE YOUR CHILD?

Don't think that a child is ignoring what is said to him if he shows no reaction or withdraws into his own world. You are not being ignored. It is much like being in a crowd and hearing people speak to each other—you know when it applies to you. To this child, the voice has no meaning and does not apply to him.

During early intervention, you will have a good idea of how well your child's receptive speech is operating.

Children who have learned the appropriate use of the words *mommy, daddy, hungry,* and the like are beginning to understand that these words have a use. They are learning to understand how that usage applies to them. A child such as this will understand "pick up your toys" and "don't touch that." If a child does not turn in response to hearing her own name, does not have the ability to name certain objects after seeing them, or disregards verbal commands, there is a receptive speech problem.

Improving Understanding

A speech therapist will most likely be working with your child if he lacks the ability to understand language. Other therapists will also dovetail their therapy with the speech therapist's exercises with the common goal of showing your child that language is useful. Children do not resist speech when they have autism, as was commonly thought years ago. It is to their advantage to understand and use speech; they just can't. It is as if there is a gap between the ears and the brain, almost as though a piece of electrical equipment has shorted out.

You, too, will be working with your child at home. In everything you and your family do, you will be showing her that language is something she can participate in. She will learn with your help. If your child is totally or essentially nonverbal, go slowly. Big picture books are helpful, as are flashcards. Avoid teaching conceptual words. If you try to explain "big" versus "small" with examples, your child may become confused. A big dog? So, is the word *dog* or *big* what is being taught? Stick with nouns until receptive language skills begin and you have a foundation. Pronouns are also very difficult to understand when receptive speech skills are poor. Use people's names or speak in the third person to help comprehension.

Clarifying Expressive Speech

Expressive speech is using words and language verbally to communicate a concept or thought. If a person has expressive speech, they have some degree of receptive speech. Children learn their expressive speech by imitation; by receiving receptively from their parents, they learn how to use language as a tool. The first words a baby says are actually a sign that receptive speech has been working effectively for quite some time.

DID YOU KNOW?

Pronouns are conceptual and should not be used unless a child has advanced speaking abilities. Speaking in the third person will be less confusing and frustrating. It is hard for a child with autism to understand that others have their own thoughts, and it's even more confusing when pronouns are used.

Encouraging a child to speak is good, but forcing him to talk is stressful and not wise. Many parents will say, "How do I encourage without forcing?" There is a fine line between the two, but after some time it will become second nature. Hold up a cookie or something your child loves to eat and say "cookie." He will not repeat it right away, but eventually he will. When he does, give him the cookie and praise him. Some children respond well to applause; others do not like the noise. The phrase "good job" is soon recognized as praise. The important thing is not to withhold the cookie because he doesn't say the word. Remember, expressive and receptive speech are tied closely together and safety and security are learned through communication. Continue meeting his needs and wants as though he was speaking and he will begin to see the usefulness of language.

Learning Sign Language

Sign language is the preferred language for people who lack verbal communication ability. American Sign Language (ASL) is the third most commonly used language in the United States. Only English and Spanish are spoken more than sign language.

The beauty of sign language is that it is convenient, portable, doesn't require any special equipment, and is standard throughout the United States. The major disadvantage—and this is one that can and should be overcome—is that the language has to be learned by all family members, not just the child with autism.

American Sign Language

There are two major forms of sign language. The most widely known through the deaf community is ASL. ASL is a consistent language used to allow people with deafness to "hear" the same things the rest of the population can hear. Speeches, concerts, plays, and many other public events have an ASL interpreter present for translation. ASL is consistent all over the United States.

Many communities have sign language classes. If you decide to use sign language in your family, these classes are helpful to teach you in an orderly way so that you can pass this along to your children and work with your autistic child with ease. In addition, books, videotapes, and computer programs are handy tools for parents and siblings of the child learning sign language.

Exact English

The other sign language, usually preferred by the autistic community, is Exact English. Exact English is based on ASL but has some important differences that make this the preferred method. The learning curve is a little easier than ASL, but the difference is not significant. If you know ASL, you can work with Exact English very easily. Learning ASL will only make Exact English easier, so don't hesitate to get instruction in ASL. A book with the Exact English signs will show the differences and should be all the extra help, beyond learning ASL, that you might need.

A BETTER PARENTING PRACTICE

Check on the Internet for books on sign language. Some excellent books have large drawings of each sign and have signs arranged in alphabetical order. This is a quick way to reference a sign if you have forgotten it. It is also a good way to learn new signs.

The primary difference between Exact English and ASL is the use of conceptual thinking. Keeping in mind that sign language was developed for a community that had full receptive speech, the motions and gestures of ASL were created to say as much as possible quickly and economically. Entire phrases are often one single sign, and many of these phrases include words that are conceptual in nature. "I love you," for example, can be said three different ways: spelling out the letters of each of the three words (eight signs), signing one sign per word (three signs), or by using one sign that represents the entire phrase. ASL uses one sign for the entire phrase whereas Exact English uses one sign per word. This is helpful for children with autism as they learn about conceptual ideas. Love is not something we can photograph or demonstrate; it is an idea that we understand, and it is an idea that takes a long time to understand for a child with autism.

Another advantage to Exact English for parents is the gradual learning of the signs. As a child learns a new sign, parents can also learn the same sign. The alphabet can easily be learned by the entire family and can be used to spell out words if a child is prone to understanding words specifically by reading. This is a way to bring words off the paper and into everyday usage.

It is very common for a child to learn a sign and then verbalize the word that the sign represents. However, this is not always the case, and the goal of sign language should not be for the child to achieve spoken language. But, if this is the case with your child, this will be an opportunity to develop more language skills. It is doubtful that your child will be able to leave signing behind altogether, but as verbalization accompanies the signs, your child's skills in receptive communication will improve along with expressive speech.

Considering Communication Boards

Many styles of communication boards are helpful for a person with autism. The options range from complex computer programs to systems as simple to operate as a set of flashcards. There are communication systems you can purchase and some you can make at home. Each child will have his own needs, and the most important issue is to personalize the board to meet those needs.

Picture Exchange Communication System (PECS)

It is common for children on the autism spectrum who have limited or no verbal ability to learn communication with a communication board. This is a form of augmentative and alternative communication (AAC). The beauty of this tool is that the learning curve is very low, and it can be used immediately. They say that a picture is worth a thousand words, and without a doubt, this is true for this form of communication.

Also known as picture communication system (PCS), this is the most widely used form of communication board used for children and adults with autism.

All that is necessary are photographs or drawings that represent people and things (nouns), actions (verbs), and concepts such as size and color (adjectives). This system is favored because of its ease of use. One downside is that as a person's vocabulary grows, more and more cards are added to the collection and they can become unwieldy. However, systems that organize cards into categories make utilization of many cards easier. It can also be difficult for a child to learn concepts from cards; if a card has a blue circle, is he communicating the color or the shape?

Building a Communication Board

If you choose to use PECS, you can test it out very easily with your child. Take photographs, or cut pictures out of magazines, and laminate them. Laminating machines to use at home can be purchased for $20 to $30 and are always handy to have around. Laminate about ten to fifteen cards, each one just a few inches square. Attach the cards together with a loose-leaf ring (without the notebook—these rings can be purchased separately) and show them to your child. As she learns that pointing to the picture of the television tells you she wishes to watch a program, she will learn the value of these cards. Make the cards relevant to your child's life so they are uniquely her own. Put them in a fanny pack and have her wear it so she has constant access to the cards.

If this is a comfortable method that works well for your child, there are more sophisticated systems available (see Appendix B). There are many ways to use PECS and they will open your child's world in a remarkable way. You are limited only by your own creativity and how you develop it for your child's needs.

Alternative Communication Methods

One method of communication that is very effective for accuracy is the keyboard. Many people with autism who cannot speak are very efficient readers and writers. They may not be able to say that they are thirsty and need a drink of water, but they are able to type it out on a simple word processing program. Even a simple text file on a desktop computer, a laptop, or handheld computer device will work. If your child seems to understand language (receptive speech) and reads, try typing a simple question. "What is your name?" is a good one to start with. He may look at you, unsure of what you want. Say the question while you point to the words on the screen and then point to the keyboard. If he understands how to communicate through writing, he will attempt to provide the answer. Coach him a bit as you begin. If your child can use this as a tool, you will know very quickly.

DID YOU KNOW?

Be certain when you create a system that you have copies and records of the cards that your child uses. If a card is lost or if you upgrade to a more sophisticated system, you will want to maintain the consistency of the same picture. Building this on a computer will make your life easier; create a file that

has all of the pictures that are being used. Back it
up on a floppy or CD, and put it somewhere safe.

If you elect to use keyboard communication, consider a handheld computer device. They are portable
and have small word processing programs that can
operate either with a small keyboard on the device or
with handwriting recognition programs using a stylus.
There is an added benefit of having a calendar on the
small computer; most people with autism instinctively
understand calendars and clocks and will use them to
maintain their schedule and routine. It is also possible
to play games on a handheld computer, which can be a
great deal of fun and a good distraction for times when
a child might be bored.

A very controversial communication tool is the
method of facilitated communication (FC). This technique operates by another person assisting a nonverbal
person's efforts in communication. The support may be
as simple as providing encouragement to boost the self-
confidence of someone who is unable to speak. It can
also involve steadying or guiding a hand to pictures or
words if necessary; people with tremors, nerve damage,
or poor muscle control may require some physical assistance. The point of contention with FC is whether a
facilitator may influence what is being communicated.
Opinions vary widely and parents who are considering
this form of communication would be wise to research
it thoroughly to reassure themselves on their choice.

Chapter 5

Putting Together an Early Intervention Team

Ten Things You Will Learn in This Chapter

- What professionals should make up your early intervention team
- What to ask when interviewing a physician
- That psychologists do more than treat mental illness
- Why an approach with combined therapies is best
- When to involve a physical therapist
- How the occupational therapist can be the most pivotal member of the team
- The details of Neuro-Immune Dysfunction Syndrome (NIDS) protocol
- Why vitamin B6 is a popular treatment option
- The possible connection between autism and celiac disease
- When to trust yourself as a parent when doctors are involved

The Members of Your Team

The most important step a parent can take to help their child with autism is to begin early intervention. If various therapies and treatments can begin before the age of three, the development of a child with autism is greatly enhanced. Your child's potential abilities will be expanded as she matures, and she will learn to relate to others in a way that did not happen before early intervention became the norm. Early intervention involves physicians, therapists, and school staff, as well as parents, of course.

Although everyone agrees that finding a good physician can make all the difference to a family stricken by autism, they will also agree that it is very difficult to find one who knows anything about autism. A smart doctor will admit it if she isn't well informed on the topic and will refer you to a specialist, or she will make an effort to learn all she can to benefit her patients. Throughout your child's growing years, you will likely have contact with several different physicians.

The Pediatrician

Pediatricians are specialists who care for the needs of children. They see children from birth to age twenty-one and beyond in certain circumstances.

Pediatrics is a specialty of medicine, as children are not just miniature adults—their health needs and issues are different and must be treated differently than an adult would be treated. Pediatricians have eleven years of college and training behind them: eight years of college and medical school, one year in pediatric internship, and two years in pediatric residency.

A pediatrician should possess many qualities, but some of the most important for your family are a kind nature, gentleness, the ability to relate to nonverbal children, and a lot of patience. Pediatricians must be involved in keeping your child well, not just treating him when he is sick.

DID YOU KNOW?

A good pediatrician will take the time to learn about your entire family. He or she will ask about your life, marriage, and health. It is not prying but rather it is a way to understand the environment in which your child lives and how it affects his health and well-being.

Selecting the right pediatrician for your child is important. It is important that you feel comfortable with this physician. Many parents feel that a team exists to raise their child and the pediatrician is one of the most valued members of that team. The pediatrician should feel the same way about your child. Begin by speaking with family and friends, and of course your support group; collect a list of names and organize yourself to find the best physician you can.

The Pediatric Neurologist

Neurology is the study of brain and nervous system disorders. Pediatric neurologists are highly specialized in both neurology and pediatrics and have all of the training of both fields, plus specialty fellowship training. They treat conditions from headaches to brain tumors and are likely to be able to make the final diagnosis of autism.

A pediatric neurologist will not be the source of primary care for your child. In other words, don't call his office for a sore throat or rash. However, if your child has some coexisting conditions such as a seizure disorder, you will be working closely with this physician for many years. He or she should have a special interest in autism and have other patients with autism. A physician who is aggressively pursuing continuing education regarding autism would be your best choice, as information on autism changes daily.

The Child Psychiatrist or Psychologist

It is hard to not balk when you are advised to consult with a child psychiatrist or psychologist. To keep this in the proper light, remember that mental health professionals do more than work with mental illness; they have a unique understanding of how structural brain disorders affect behavior and how best to treat those problems. There is a definite relationship between the mind, body, and spirit, and a psychiatrist works in those somewhat nebulous areas.

A psychiatrist is a physician who has had additional training studying the brain and the mind. He or she will have twelve to sixteen years of training. The psychiatrist can prescribe medications, whereas other experts in mental health cannot. A child psychiatrist will work to determine how all aspects of a person's life are affecting his or her health; this includes physical, emotional, educational, developmental, and social issues. A child psychiatrist can also be helpful as a family adjusts to the diagnosis of autism.

A clinical psychologist will have either a master's or doctorate. They are not physicians but work closely with many physician specialties to coordinate the use of medication from the physician and counseling from the psychologist. They can make a recommendation to the child's physician that a particular medication be used. Psychologists will often work with an entire family to modify undesirable behaviors in a child with autism.

Selecting the Right Physician

The first thing to do is organize your list by geographical convenience; it matters little how good a particular physician may be if you can't get there. You don't need to be in your doctor's backyard, but in an emergency, it is nice to have a doctor a few minutes away. It is possible the physician may have more than one office if it is a large practice, in which case knowing what days the doctor is in is helpful. While you are mapping out locations, it is helpful to make a note of what hours the office is open. Many offices will be open in the evening one night a week to accommodate working parents.

A BETTER PARENTING PRACTICE

All professionals in mental health fields should be pursuing additional study on various issues in the ever-changing health care field. Look for a psychiatrist or psychologist with a special interest in autism. If the doctor regularly deals with autism, the condition will be familiar to her, which will result in better care for your child.

Next, decide if you prefer a male or female physician. It may not matter to you or you may feel more comfortable with a physician of the same sex as your child. If you would be more comfortable with a physician of a certain age, write that in too. Older doctors have more experience but younger doctors may be more open and innovative; it depends on the personality of the physician. If you are uncomfortable asking someone's age, ask how many years he or she has been in practice.

Then begin interviewing. Call the office to set up an appointment, which should be a free-of-charge visit; tell the receptionist that you would like to schedule a "get acquainted" visit as you are choosing a physician for your child. Note the attitude of the staff on the telephone—in the future, those will be the first people you speak with. They should be friendly, helpful, and professional.

The physician, when you meet her, should be open and interested in your questions. She should feel no discomfort at being quizzed about child care and development, and how she handles situations that you ask about. Ask questions specific to your concerns about autism to determine the doctor's level of experience with and interest in ASD. The physician will likely have questions for you, too, and setting up this dialogue is important for the future of your working relationship.

The Importance of Qualified Therapists

Medical care may be only as good as the ancillary medical professionals that provide it. Different therapists will see your child more than his physician will and it is important that they are qualified, knowledgeable, and interested in their field. You should be able to tell if the therapists you are seeing care about their work; checking their qualifications is also very easy.

Speech Therapists and Audiologists

Audiologists are the head of the team that diagnoses and handles hearing disorders. They also diagnose and recommend treatment for many communication disorders. When a child has autism, an audiologist is frequently the first medical professional who sees the child, because the parents suspect deafness. Audiologists have at least a master's degree.

DID YOU KNOW?

Audiologists are trained to work with very young children and nonverbal children. They will use several techniques to determine if a child has a hearing disorder or a receptive language problem. Although they do not diagnose autism, they are important for ruling out a disorder such as deafness.

Speech therapists, or speech and language patholo-
gists, work with people who have many varied kinds of
hearing or communication problems. In an average day,
a speech therapist may see a child with a lisp, an older
person who has had a stroke, a nonverbal child with
autism, and a person with deafness. They work with
people of all ages.

Speech therapists are considered by many physicians
and parents to be the primary therapist that coordinates
all the therapy for the child with autism. Because they
work with swallowing disorders as well as speech problems, they can coordinate therapies with physical, occupational, and sensory therapy to achieve the maximum
results in the time they have with a child. An approach
that combines therapies helps a child put order into his
disordered world.

As your child begins therapy, regardless of what
method you decide on, you will likely interact with a
speech therapist. Talk to the therapist about your concerns regarding language development and what you
can do at home to reinforce the therapy. Many small
things that you do on a day-to-day basis can incorpo-
rate the therapy that is being used to help your child
progress.

Physical Therapists

Whether or not your child sees a physical therapist (PT) will depend on her gross motor skills. Many
children with autism do not have any deficits in this
area and physical therapy is not necessary, but others have extensive issues, and the PT may coordinate

all the therapies a child receives. The goal of physical therapy is to improve functioning. Issues such as range of motion and flexibility are primary concerns that will be addressed by the therapist. PTs work to increase a patient's independence by increasing balance, coordination, and strength.

If your physician recommends a PT, you may find your first visit with him or her to be much like a doctor visit. PTs will analyze a patient's medical history, do an evaluation of their own, and recommend a course of treatment. They will develop an appropriate therapy plan, coordinate all forms of therapy, and instruct parents on home activities to enforce the treatment plan. They may have an assistant work with the patient, but this is not always the case.

DOES THIS SOUND LIKE YOUR CHILD?

Many daily living skills are difficult for children with autism to perform. The lack of language, either receptive or expressive, creates difficulty for a child when she isn't sure of what she is to do or how to do it. An occupational therapist will work with a child to increase fine motor skills but also to increase reasoning and understanding.

PTs are college educated, with a minimum of a master's degree being preferred by most employers. Some states require only a bachelor's degree. They will be certified and belong to a variety of organizations. Continuing education is also a requirement for licensure. As with any kind of therapist, a special interest in autism is helpful.

Occupational Therapists

One of the most important professionals your child will interact with will be the occupational therapist (OT). This person will be pivotal in helping your child build skills or compensate for skills to perform in normal everyday life. The OT may also be referred to as a sensory integration therapist. Like all other therapists your child will work with, this person is college educated, is involved with continuing education, and will belong to one or more professional organizations.

An OT will work with a child to teach her to use various tools in her life. All of the skills taught enforce different aspects of mental function. A variety of activities will be involved over the course of a child's therapy:

- Using a computer
- Using paper and pencil/crayons
- Playing video games to teach hand-eye coordination
- Various exposures to sensory stimuli to decrease overstimulation problems
- Repetitive activities to teach sequencing
- Flashcards and other language aids in connection with speech therapy

An OT will do a wide variety of things to increase your child's ability to function independently. If you need something to help your child compensate or adapt, ask the OT. If classroom equipment needs to be modified, the OT will know how to do it. Problem solving is their specialty, and they will bring many solutions to situations that puzzle you.

Licensed Clinical Social Workers

The licensed clinical social worker (LCSW) is no longer exclusively for families who have financial or social problems. The LCSW is a mental health professional that deals with a variety of emotional and societal issues that bring about conflicts in life. LCSWs are college educated with a master's degree and are required to complete continuing education annually.

If a psychologist can be viewed as treating the mental health of an individual, the LCSW can be considered as the mental health expert for society. They specialize in maintaining the social functioning of an individual in a group. Whether it be family, a group home, or society in general, the LCSW's goal is to create the best social situation possible for your child.

Social workers can be helpful when an adult child is considered for placement in a group home environment. A LCSW will also help a family determine if they are getting the financial help they are entitled to and that it is distributed properly if that is a concern. They can help a family with many issues at the school level as well. LCSW see people with autism every day and they know the community as well as their clients, and they can assist in making the best decisions for both.

Possible Treatment Programs

As you explore various options for your child's medical care, you will find many programs and treatment plans. Investigate ideas that are sound, and research all you need. But remember, there is no cure for autism. Your goal is to make your child the best person that he can be, which is a goal you will be able to reach.

There are many good treatment plans. If you are interested in any form of treatment, consult with your child's physician. It is also helpful to speak with other parents at your support group meeting. Don't try to reinvent the wheel; other people can provide you with a great deal of information. But remember that you must follow your own instincts and do what you think is best for your child and family.

Neuro-Immune Dysfunction Syndrome (NIDS) Protocol

Research has suggested a link between autoimmune disorders, autism, and ADD. NIDS (Neuro-Immune Dysfunction Syndrome) treatment protocol operates to balance the immune system in an effort to reduce the symptoms of autism. It is considered a form of complementary or alternative medicine therapy by the American Academy of Pediatrics.

The treatment protocol involves looking for various markers including allergens, and viral and bacterial titers. For the patient's family, this means that blood and urine are analyzed for things that the child may be allergic to or that may indicate levels of exposure to certain viruses and/or bacterial infections. If different disease processes appear, or allergies are determined, treatment can begin that may alleviate some of the symptoms of autism. Treatment then can begin with allergy medications, antifungals, antivirals, and SSRIs (medications used for depression, anxiety, and the control of obsessive-compulsive behaviors). People on the NIDS protocol are monitored closely with monthly or bimonthly blood work.

Applied Behavioral Analysis (ABA)

Applied behavioral analysis (ABA), also known as the Lovaas method, is one of the most popular forms of treatment of autism. This therapy does not attempt to reverse a medical condition but has been created instead to change undesirable behaviors into desirable ones. It also teaches social skills, life skills, and encourages language. It builds on small skills, creating bigger skills, and teaching motivation for learning. ABA claims to be effective in modifying the behavior of up to 50 percent of children with autism to the point that they were able to attend a normal classroom without paraprofessional assistance.

A BETTER PARENTING PRACTICE

Don't ever begin two or more therapies simultaneously. If you have positive results, you will never be certain which treatment was the effective one. Give a new therapy at least three months before you evaluate the results and then decide if you wish to continue.

ABA is not without controversy. Some fear that children are simply responding to verbal or nonverbal cues and that the behavior mechanizes them. Proponents say that isn't the case if the child is taught properly. There is also a misconception that aversive therapy is used as punishment for undesirable behaviors, when in fact it is not. Unfortunately there is no way to determine which children will be the most responsive and successful with ABA, but younger children who spend more than thirty hours each week in ABA therapy have shown the best results. It requires a great deal of structure within the family but results begin to show quickly, and it is an ideal therapy for many children and their families.

The GFCF Diet

One of the most popular treatment plans involves the use of a gluten-free, casein-free (GFCF) diet. This means exactly what it says: There are no glutens or casein ingested by a person on this diet. It excludes all wheat, rye, barley, and oats from the diet as well as almost all milk products. Many parents maintain their children on this diet, and report positive results. Although scientific studies are lacking, parental success votes in with an amazing 80 percent rate of satisfaction with the treatment plan.

The premise of eliminating gluten and casein from the diet involves a theory that autism could potentially be a metabolic disorder or an autoimmune disease. It is suspected that the body may be having a toxicological response to the molecule of gluten, and that the central nervous system (CNS) behavior is affected by the action of the molecule in a body that cannot tolerate it. Because the structure of the casein molecule is similar to that of gluten, it is also included in the elimination diet. This is very similar to celiac sprue (also called celiac disease or nontropical sprue), an autoimmune disease.

If you decide to begin this approach to autism, do your homework first. Many products have hidden gluten in them, and even one molecule can affect the success of the diet.

Vitamin B6

Vitamin B6 is a very popular form of treatment. Individuals require different levels of vitamin B6, and if a person has a deficiency, the theory goes, taking large doses of the vitamin will assist them. If that is the case, autism could also be viewed as a vitamin deficiency, much like scurvy resulting from a lack of vitamin C. The key is balancing the B6 intake with the other vitamins to utilize B6 efficiently without causing a deficiency in another vitamin, which could cause undesirable side effects. Magnesium is used to counteract the larger B6 intake and has shown to be effective as well.

DID YOU KNOW?

Vitamin B6 therapy has been shown to improve eye contact, reduce self-stimulating behaviors, reduce tantrums, improve social and environmental interactions, and improve speech. If you are interested in this therapy, contact the Autism Research Institute. Your physician may not know about this therapy;

brochures from the institute have more information
and will help explain the details.

B6 therapy is not a cure—the founders of the treatment will be the first to admit that. But with studies
showing at least half of children responding favorably to
megadoses of vitamins B6 and normal supplements of
vitamin B complex and magnesium, it is not something
parents can easily disregard.

Working with the Experts

When patients feel the doctor, or therapist, has knowledge they could not possibly understand, and they trust
without question any advice, treatment, or medication
given, a problem is just brewing. Meeting with physicians and therapists as an equal, as a member of a team
all working toward the same goal, is the approach that
will help your child the most.

As a mom or dad, you are with your child twenty-
four hours a day, seven days a week (with the excep-
tion of school hours and other short times away). Constantly you are monitoring and observing his behavior;
you notice the smallest of changes and can sense his
emotions. And you are the only one who does that.

Trusting yourself is the most important part of any
therapy or treatment. No one knows your child as you
do and you can rely on your instincts. Always collect
advice and listen to the experience of others, but when
it comes time for the decision, you are qualified to
make it.

Chapter 6

ASD and Effects on the Family

Ten Things You Will Learn in This Chapter

- Divorce rates for parents of disabled children
- Differences between a mother's reaction to diagnosis and a father's reaction
- How the five stages of life are different for a child with autism
- Why it's important to keep autism from becoming your focus
- What intimacy really means
- How to re-energize your marriage
- Autism's impact on older siblings
- How to keep a younger sibling from growing up too fast
- Normal sibling reactions to diagnosis
- How to keep siblings from becoming isolated

ASD and Your Marriage

It is estimated that 50 to 75 percent of marriages fail if a disabled child is in the family. Exact statistics vary widely depending on the source, but the numbers are always high. It is a fact: Having a child with autism is hard on a marriage and a family. It is difficult for a couple, particularly when they are young, to remain a couple and have a child who is so far from what they had anticipated.

Further, other people become so involved with your life, such as doctors, therapists, teachers, and social workers, that it feels they have become part of your marriage. It is hard to remember that you are still the same two people who fell in love, married, and planned to live happily ever after.

How Mom Is Affected

Pregnancy is an exciting time for a woman. The growing child within her—as it begins to move and kick and then show a silhouette on an ultrasound—is the person she most anticipates meeting. It doesn't matter if it is a first child or the second or the tenth. This baby is the focus of all her thoughts.

When the baby is born and the doctor announces whether it is a boy or girl, invariably the first question heard is, "Is everything all right?" And what a relief it is when all ten fingers and toes are present and there are no disabilities. A healthy child has come into the world.

It is a shock to a mom when she sees the developmental progress made by her child beginning to slip away slowly. Her beautiful baby, now approaching the toddler stage, with his few words and joyful reactions to the world around him, is changing. The words are fewer and fewer until they are heard no more. The interactive baby, who chuckled and had sparkling eyes just looking at Mom, now seems enclosed in a world of darkness where no one else can go.

Her child will no longer look at her, no longer try to learn new words or even use the already learned ones, and doesn't seem to hear her.

There are usually five stages in a child's life. But the stages are different when your child has autism.

- Infant—The hopes, dreams, and visions of a new life are shattered with the realization that something has gone wrong.
- Toddler—The realization begins to sink in that what was wrong isn't going away and must be coped with.
- Young school age—More dreams are lost as a child enters school and Mom can see the contrast between her child and other children.
- Older school age—Progress is made but concerns begin over challenges brought by puberty, adolescence, and the beginning of young adulthood.
- Adult—As the child becomes an adult, Mom becomes aware that she, too, is aging and she begins to worry what will happen to her child when she is gone.

This is a lot for a young mother to absorb. And moms do think through all five stages within a few months of the diagnosis. Stress, fear, denial, anxiety, confusion, anger, depression, and sadness are inevitable. It may be one of the hardest times in a mother's life.

Diagnosis and Adjustment

Mothers are deeply affected when the process of diagnosing their child begins. The protective and maternal instincts within a mother are natural, so her resentment toward all the "experts" who have suddenly intruded right into the middle of her family's life is normal.

DID YOU KNOW?

Mothers may feel especially frustrated when the experts can't give a diagnosis within a day or two. The testing for autism and the other related conditions can take quite some time, and frustration with medical personnel is also normal. The acceptance that will eventually come is at this point a long time off, and it is a tumultuous time.

Eventually all of the emotions that run amok within a mom will settle down, and although none of them ever disappear entirely, they become manageable and a sense of acceptance occurs. Mom will begin to accept that this is the situation and will begin to reset goals and plans, accommodating her child's needs and abilities within that framework. There will always be times when she feels sad or depressed; she will have spikes of anger at the situation when a problem arises that isn't easily solved, but she will have learned to accept and do what moms do best: love.

How Dad Is Affected

Dads are also affected by the realization that their child has been diagnosed on the autism spectrum, but the reactions of a father are different than those of a mother. A mom needs to be aware that the reactions of her partner, although different, are normal.

- Infant—When a dad has a new infant, his pride and delight are unparalleled. When something goes wrong, it is hard for fathers to come to terms with the disability and they may take a long time to accept it. Usually a father grapples with acceptance longer than a mother.
- Toddler—Realization begins to force its way into a father's mind. Fathers will either react with acceptance of the problem and begin to find ways to solve it, or they will deny the problem exists and look to place blame with someone. Denial is a common reaction for men because they feel responsible for the events that occur within their family.
- Young school age—As a child enters school, fathers begin to see the deficits and often have trouble seeing the progress. It is important for therapists, physicians, and the child's mother to point out the progress being made so that the father can see the glass as half full. This stage

is normal, and it will pass. Again, dads feel
responsible and frustrated that they can't fix the
problem.

- Older school age—This is a time where fathers
really shine if they have come to acceptance,
which most have by this stage. The progress is
evident and now the issues are ones that men
handle well. There are specific challenges to be
met and problem solving is the needed skill.
Dad will find his problem-solving skills to be
very useful and he will feel less like a failure and
more like a dad.
- Adult—Like Mom, Dad becomes aware that his
child has become an adult and that he will not
always be there to protect his son or daughter.
Most likely, he has started estate and financial
planning to protect his child, but he will work
on solving the issues that will face his child even
after Mom and he are gone.

Dad has a lot to absorb, just as Mom does. Men
have different coping mechanisms than women do, so
they will process and absorb all of this differently. It is
important for Mom to remember that Dad's method of
dealing with the diagnosis of their child is no less valid
than her method. It may seem that a man isn't handling
the situation well, and perhaps there is some denial
involved, but given time the acceptance will occur.

Keeping ASD from Becoming Your Life

The strongest piece of advice most therapists will give a couple that has a child with autism is "Do not allow autism to become your entire life." It is so easy to begin to eat, breathe, and sleep autism, but it will do no good—not for you, not for your spouse, and not even for your child. There is enough stress within a marriage to begin with, and adding autism to the mix only ratchets up that level of stress.

A BETTER PARENTING PRACTICE

When you are speaking with your spouse, you shouldn't say the words "you never" or "you always." Your spouse has different thoughts and approaching a conversation with "I feel" is the way to begin. It is possible your spouse is unaware of the problem and gentle communication will solve the problem.

Although your child has autism or another disorder on the spectrum, you still have control of your life. If you allow ASD to become your entire life, you will socially isolate yourself. Turn to each other for support and go to events, support groups, and other activities as a couple to strengthen your bond. You can become stronger because of autism and not allow it to unravel your marriage. It just takes a little time, effort, and a lot of love.

Maintaining and Creating Intimacy

One of the most difficult things in a marriage, let alone a marriage with a disabled child, is maintaining the intimacy that is unique to marriage. When a couple goes from being a man and a woman to being a mom and a dad, they often find it hard to remember they are still a man and a woman! The special intimacy that you knew before you had a child is just as important, perhaps even more important, than it was before. It is important to remember that intimacy is not always about sex. So how do you keep intimacy alive when you have children, and especially a child with special needs?

- Go out on a date with each other. Schedule an actual date, go out, and talk about anything but autism.
- Celebrate every occasion you can think of. Anniversaries of the first date, first kiss, first anything—just celebrate!
- Splurge on gifts for each other. You don't have to have a reason other than the fact that you love each other.
- Buy books on intimacy and sexuality. Have grandma watch the kids and go to a hotel for an evening. Enjoy each other like it was the first time.
- Give each other massages with no sexuality expected. Just make the other person relax and feel good.

- Plan a picnic and lie on the ground looking at the clouds. Tell each other what you see in the clouds.
- Whether or not you believe it, pretend. If you reincarnate into another life, what will each of you be?
- Remember, you are still the same woman and the same man who fell in love and got married. ASD has not changed that.

It isn't that hard to keep the spark alive or to relight it if the years have allowed the flame to go out. Remember, the child who has brought some extra challenges—and yes, some stress as well—into your lives is a product of the love you have for each other. This child can only benefit from the closeness that you as a couple will have by the efforts you make to keep your intimate life alive.

ASD and the Effects on Siblings

Autism affects everyone in the family. Perhaps no one feels this effect more than the siblings of the ASD child. Parents of the child on the spectrum are often so wrapped up in the issues surrounding autism, and understandably so, that they overlook the ways autism is affecting their other children. It isn't bad parenting; it is human nature. Raising children is a balancing act for parents as they try to meet everyone's needs and provide a complete childhood for each of their children.

Older Siblings

When an older child or a teenager has a new sibling, it is enough of an adjustment. Adding autism into the mixture a couple of years later makes this adjustment even more challenging. A child who is ten years older (or more) than the new arrival will view the family dynamics differently than a younger child.

If there are a significant number of years separating the older sibling from the child with autism, the younger child may not have much impact on the daily life of the older child. This is especially true if the older child is in high school, for example, and nearly ready to move out of the house to live on her own or to go to college. The older child may not be much involved with the daily trials of living with a child with autism.

However, the older sibling may have some concerns that other children don't think of. The older child likely recognizes fairly quickly that autism is going to be around for the rest of her life, and she may already be concerned about her role in taking care of an adult with autism in several years. This will impact not only her life but the life of her future spouse and any children they may have as well. Autism affects everyone in a family.

Slightly Older Siblings

When a child has a sibling that is two to eight years younger and that child is diagnosed with autism or another spectrum disorder, it can affect the sibling(s) in several different ways. Children have their own personalities and how they react in a given situation will depend on their personality. There is no one way children handle issues in their lives, but there are some generalizations that can be made. Understanding the mechanisms behind observed behaviors can assist you in helping your other children. Typical reactions can include the following:

- A sibling acts as another parent.
- A sibling pulls away from the family.
- A sibling attempts to "make up" for autism by being a "model" child.
- A sibling establishes his or her own identity through flamboyant behavior.
- A sibling struggles with anxiety or depression.
- A sibling feels resentment toward the child with autism.

Although this list is by no means all-inclusive, most siblings of children with ASD will fall into one of these categories. Just when autism itself seems overwhelming and more than any person can emotionally handle, the realization that the other children have developed needs because of their younger sibling can overwhelm the most patient of parents. But it is, in reality, a simple process of identifying the issues and addressing them one by one; tackling the entire situation at once isn't going to work. Dealing with one issue, one crisis, one dilemma at a time will work with a little practice.

Parents will often report that they observe two of the behaviors in the previous list more commonly than other behaviors. Most of the siblings of a child who is on the spectrum will take one of two roles. They will either fall into the role of an "alternative" parent or isolate themselves from the family and autism as far as humanly possible.

The Parental Sibling

Children who begin to act as another parent have both positive and negative issues to deal with. The positive side is the child's acceptance and involvement in the family. As that child matures into an adult, he will have a compassion for people with disabilities; it is not something that is foreign to him as it is to many people. The downside is that the parents might rely on such a child heavily, and it is possible for that child to lose his own childhood in the process.

DOES THIS SOUND LIKE YOUR CHILD?

Children who are used to their sibling with autism not participating in games are thrilled when interaction and participation begins. They also can become jealous because of the attention focused on the child with autism. Don't forget to praise your other children for their skills and achievements.

Parents need to be aware of a child who becomes parental. It isn't a behavior to be discouraged, as families should work together and look out for each other. But it is important not to let a child take on so much responsibility that he becomes overwhelmed and loses himself in the process. A child who observes her younger sibling about to poke a fork in an electrical outlet and stops him is a good thing. A child who feels she is responsible for everything that the child with autism does, and carries the guilt of an accident or problem, is a bad thing.

Younger Siblings

When a child is born to a family that already has a child with autism, there are different issues to deal with. There is no adjustment period for the nonautistic child—he has never known his sibling as being anything other than autistic. The element of adjustment is removed, but other challenges remain.

Most children who have a sibling that is one or two years younger have much of the same issues as any siblings that are close in age, but magnified. A child with autism, because of the very nature of ASD, demands more time, patience, and tolerance than a child without the disorder would ever have. The major problem? A child without the disorder can "get lost." It is so easy to postpone the needs of a "normal" child because of the heavy demands of an ASD child.

Jealousy and Resentment

It is important that parents go the extra mile to avoid jealousy and resentment from the child who is not autistic. Jealousy is a problem that begins subtly, but when the children reach their teenage years, it can become a serious problem. Resentment is the result of jealousy, and a resentful teenager is a problem waiting to happen. The teenage years are challenge enough without having undesirable behaviors surface as attempts to gain attention occur. You can watch for signs in your children indicating that jealousy and resentment may be becoming an issue. A child may

- Request that Mom and Dad attend school functions alone (without the child with autism attending)
- Feel concern or embarrassment about having his or her friends visit for sleepovers or other activities
- Become more in need of physical contact with one or both parents, wanting closeness such as cuddling
- Express jealousy overtly (the phrase "But he gets to . . ." is a definite sign of jealousy)
- Excessively argue about chores and responsibilities
- Show behavior that indicates an obsession with his or her health

It is also important to watch for competitive behavior. Competitiveness may be the first sign of jealousy. A child who goes out of her way to show the parents accomplishments and skills may be feeling that the child with autism is getting a lot of positive feedback for reaching what is perceived to be very small goals.

Parental Siblings and Isolated Siblings

The baby boomer generation is dovetailing careers and family. Because of this, it is common to have age gaps of ten years or more between children. If there is a child with autism in the family and another baby comes along ten years later, there are some unique issues to be faced by the family.

When a sibling is much younger than the child with autism, the younger child will never know of any adjustment that had to be made in the family. This is simply life, the way it has always been, and the way it will always be. The main risk to a sibling of a disabled child is through the maturing years.

It is very easy to inadvertently cause a child to "grow up" too quickly. The younger child starts watching out for the older because it is the natural thing to do. The burden of that responsibility is too much for a child to bear, and it may be sowing the seeds of resentment that will fully bloom later in life.

Most children realize as they approach their young adult years that this sibling with autism will be a part of their life forever. Realization strikes that someday this may be their responsibility. It isn't necessary to bring up this topic; it will arise on its own when the time is right. And it is very possible that a child with autism will eventually live in a supervised group home or even live independently.

A BETTER PARENTING PRACTICE

Negative attention is better than no attention—or so a child thinks. It is especially true for the sibling of a child with autism. If your other children begin having behavior problems, review how much individualized time they get from you. Negative behavior can be changed into a positive outcome.

Interference in childhood activities is less likely when a child is younger than his or her sibling with autism. The younger child will fit into the family's already established routine. It would be wise to find respite care so that the younger child will have time alone with parents. Involving extended family is an option that is helpful and supportive. As the family pulls together, a family life is created that is secure and comfortable for all members.

Some children will not form a parental type of attachment to their sibling with autism. This happens more commonly in children who are introverted. They attempt to put as much distance between them and their sibling and family as possible. Often, the cause is quite simple: They are tired of autism.

It is important that a child who withdraws from the family because of autism be allowed to flourish on his or her own. These children are often susceptible to depression, and it is helpful to have a therapist address the issues of this one child alone, without any mention of autism. It is very important that the parents spend time with that child alone to enjoy activities and projects that are totally unrelated to autism. Parents also need to be clear, verbally and through their actions, that they do not feel the sibling is responsible for his brother or sister. The less the child with autism impacts his sibling, the better the chances for both children to evolve a healthy relationship over time.

The Social Impact of Having an ASD Sibling

Children who have a sibling with ASD have mixed feelings about their brother or sister. At times, it affects their social life, and at other times, it is totally irrelevant. Like any sibling combination, it can be a rocky road laced with arguments and love, all at the same time. The sibling of the child with autism will claim his brother or sister as his worst enemy or best friend, depending on the day. One thing is certain: It is always an adventure!

Some of the biggest problems siblings of ASD children face are issues within their own peer group. Your child, having the experience of a sibling with a disability, has a different outlook on the world than many children have. It is not unusual for children, particularly in the middle and elementary school years, to hear other children tease or outright ridicule their sibling with autism. Parents should address this immediately, as the problem will only escalate and eventually alienate a child from her own peer group.

DID YOU KNOW?

Support groups for parents of children with autism can provide information on locating a support group for siblings. Check with your local chapter of the Autism Society of America or other organizations that have support groups. Your child needs to realize she is not alone.

If a child is being singled out because of her sibling, it is important for the parents to contact the school system. In this case, it isn't enough to tell your child to ignore the teasing, for two reasons. Your child will generally rise to the occasion to defend her sibling with autism and be on the defensive whenever interacting with her peer group. Additionally, the children doing the teasing will continue to be intolerant of people who are different from them and the cycle will continue. Do not hesitate to schedule a conference with counselors, teachers, or other school staff to address and put an end to the problem.

Chapter 7

Public School and Educational Resources

Ten Things You Will Learn in This Chapter

- Details of the Individuals with Disabilities Education Act
- What your child will learn in a special education program
- What's involved in creating an Individual Education Plan (IEP)
- The benefits and drawbacks of inclusion
- Who makes up the IEP team
- What paperwork is necessary for your child's IEP
- What happens when your child turns fourteen
- How to discover your child's interests
- There are two primary methods used to instruct children with autism
- Differences between ABA and TEACCH

What You Need to Know

In the United States, all fifty states are mandated to have early intervention programs and special education available to children. For children with autism, early intervention will most likely begin around the child's second birthday. Special education starts for children at the age of three.

The special education maze is complicated at times, and you may find yourself feeling like you're in an adversarial relationship with the school system. But never forget that you are your child's best advocate. Staying informed about political and legal issues that affect children with autism is critical to your child's successful school career.

IDEA

In the mid-1970s, a new law was enacted called the Education for All Handicapped Children Act of 1975. The federal government had finally recognized that inadequate education for children with disabilities was costing American society a great deal. In 1997, the law was given a major facelift and was renamed the Individuals with Disabilities Education Act (IDEA). Revisions were made in 2004, including some changes to the Individualized Education Program (IEP) process (multiyear IEPs, IEP attendance, and need to meet short-term objectives, etc.), due process (timelines, attorney fees, etc.), and discipline. It also worked to align the IDEA with the No Child Left Behind Act.

Title I is a federal funding program for public schools above a certain population count. IDEA requires public schools receiving Title I funding to follow two standards: All students must have available to them a free appropriate public education (FAPE), and that education must be within the least restrictive environment (LRE). This education is to be provided from ages three to twenty-two, but may have variances by individual state laws.

Navigating the Language of Special Education

Although it may feel at times as though you need to be an attorney or political science expert to understand the technicalities of the government's involvement with special education, it isn't all that difficult. Laws will come and go, change and modify, and evolve to better (hopefully) serve our children. It is important to understand the basic principles of special education laws so that when changes do occur, you as a parent will understand the effect they may have on your child.

In 2003 proposed changes to IDEA, the primary law regarding disabled students, went to congressional review. The changes that could affect students with autism center on behavioral issues related to the condition; often children with autism will have violent outbursts that make it difficult for them to get along in a group setting such as a classroom. If a child is prone to aggression, even if it is caused by his condition, he may or may not be able to continue in school depending on the outcome of the revisions to IDEA. Parents should be aware of any changes to IDEA due to its effects on the autism community.

There are many newsletters and websites that provide current information on issues in the government that can affect special education. It isn't so important that you understand and are aware of every little detail but that you know how to handle the laws if you have problems with your child's education. No one can be an expert on everything, but anyone can be an expert on finding any piece of information they may need. Avail yourself of all of the experts to stay current on congressional issues that affect the rights of disabled students.

Integration and Special Education

When a student is disabled, education includes much more than the three Rs. Beyond academic learning, students in special education programs also learn much about managing the needs of their daily life. Daily skills, such as dressing appropriately, using the toilet, self-feeding, and other hygiene needs are also taught. The needs of a student in special education are the same in some ways as what nondisabled students need, and also very different at the same time. Thus a multifaceted program, coordinated by teachers, administrators, therapists, and parents, is planned out annually. This plan is known as the Individual Education Program (IEP), which is discussed in more detail in the next section.

Least Restrictive Environments, Mainstreaming, and Inclusion

IDEA establishes that students must have access to an education in the Least Restrictive Environment (LRE). In practice, this means that a student must be placed in the same classroom she would attend if she were not disabled. Supplementary services, such as aids, support systems, and communication equipment, should be used to achieve this goal. If a student's IEP clearly shows that the regular classroom is not suitable, after thoroughly researching the use of various supports, aids, and paraprofessionals, other arrangements can be made. Inclusion, mainstreaming, and LRE all refer to the same thing.

However, IDEA has recognized that the regular classroom is not suitable for all students. A "continuum of alternative placement" is to be in place to answer to the needs of each child. This includes special education classrooms, special schools, instruction in the home environment, and in group homes or institutions.

Achieving Free Appropriate Public Education (FAPE)

FAPE is something every child in the United States is entitled to and it is a phrase very few parents know. Every child is entitled to have the best education possible, to have it be easily accessible, and with no attached fees. This includes services such as special education and "related services" necessary to fulfill the IEP goals. This mandate applies to all Title I schools and encompasses academics, physical education, and speech therapy.

Related services include hearing evaluations, speech therapy, psychological counseling, physical and occupational therapy, recreational therapy, vocational counseling, and health care counseling. This is not an all-inclusive list, as any service that is necessary for a child's success is included in this category. These are not luxuries; they are essential to acquiring the free and appropriate public education that every child is entitled to, by law, in the United States.

■ A BETTER PARENTING PRACTICE

If school staff claim a lack of personnel to provide related services, remind them of their obligation to provide FAPE. The law says that no child shall be denied services needed because of inconveniences to the school district. Your state department of education can assist you in resolving the problem.

A free and appropriate public education means that every child with a disability is in essentially the same environment as he would be were he not disabled. Least restrictive environments are part of this education and related services are as well. FAPE and LRE (or inclusion, as it is commonly known) are the tangible manifestations of IDEA.

Individual Educational Program

Individual Educational Program (IEP) is a term that you will become quite familiar with. Think of it as the road map that runs from early intervention through graduation. This plan describes in detail all special education services that will be called upon to meet the needs of your child with autism. Each IEP is different, as each student is different. It outlines goals and expectations for your child and gives you an idea of what to expect for the school year.

The IEP is a fluid plan, meaning it changes from year to year and sometimes even within the same year as different accomplishments and problems occur. It can also be thought of as a sort of contract, as it commits the school to using resources to achieve the goals the team sets. A well-done IEP also serves to eliminate misunderstandings by all of the members of the educational team. Without an IEP, there is no special education; therefore, think of this document as the single most important part of your child's education.

DID YOU KNOW?

A parent has the right to call for an IEP meeting any time he or she feels that there are needs to be addressed or revisions that should be made. Children change over a twelve-month period and the IEP may need to change as well.

Traditionally short-term goals have been a part of every IEP but the ever-evolving laws may change that at some time in the future. Long-term or annual goals in the IEP—the heart of the document—will be the baseline on which a child's education is planned. The goals that are to unfold over a twelve-month period must be reasonable, practical, and designed to strengthen a weak area that is of educational concern. It is important that these goals match well with the student's current level of performance; they should not reach too high or too low. Parents and teachers need to consider a child's abilities and how they can best enhance those for progress and maturity.

The IEP Team

The IEP team is made up of a group of people who work with you and your child to create the best education plan possible. Certain people are required to be involved, and other experts may be involved as well:

- The student—In reality, it is unlikely that your child will be included in an IEP meeting, so it is your job as the child's parent to address his desires and concerns if he has expressed them.
- The special education teacher—This individual will be the one to oversee the plan that is established in the meeting.
- A school administrator—This will be either a principal or special education director.
- An adult service agency representative—This is only required if transition services are being planned that would involve an outside agency. If it is physically impossible for someone to attend, a phone conference will suffice.
- An interpreter—This is a requirement if the parents are deaf or do not speak English.

Other teachers and therapists may be asked to join the meeting if appropriate. Parents may also request an advocate of their choosing if they wish. It is very helpful to have an advocate, particularly if you are new to the IEP process. Parents must be notified of an IEP meeting reasonably ahead of time and if the date cannot be arranged with their schedules, the IEP must be rescheduled. If a parent is unable to attend—for instance, because she is serving in the military—the school is to make alternative arrangements through phone conference or another satisfactory method that will include the parent.

The IEP Process

The first time you meet for an IEP may be intimidating. A conference is usually called by the school, but can be called by anyone who feels a meeting is necessary. This includes parents, teachers, administrators, and anyone involved (even a member of the lunchroom staff isn't out of the question if a child has dietary issues). The entire process can be unsettling to parents, as this large and structured meeting can emphasize the severity of their child's disorder. But remember that this team has been created to help your child acquire the best education possible, and you are a member of that team with equal ranking and qualification.

IDEA states that an IEP must be conducted within thirty days of when teachers and you determine that special education and other related services are necessary. IEP meetings take place at the school or a school district office and will include the entire IEP team. Paperwork will be signed by all parties to acknowledge the meeting date and time for permanent records and you will sign a form that acknowledges you have a copy of the special education laws and that you know your rights as well as those of your child.

The meeting itself involves covering all of the team's goals and expectations for your child. You and the team will go through various categories of his education, such as communication skills, and rate his current levels of performance. Goals for the next twelve months will then be established. This process will continue for each category of your child's education.

A BETTER PARENTING PRACTICE

The IEP meeting can take place without the parent present. This is a last-resort option. Parents need to be involved and the school district must go out of its way to include parents. If the parents are not in attendance, adequate documentation of efforts to include them must be recorded.

It is helpful for parents to have a list when they attend the IEP meeting. If you feel that the school should provide particular services, this is the place to discuss it. The school district needs to address issues you feel strongly about, even if it does not agree with you. For example, a school that will not provide sign language instruction at the parents' request needs to have a very good reason for not doing so. Lack of personnel or schedule concerns are not good enough reasons.

The IEP meeting can be held at any time of the school year for convenience. As it comes time to reconvene to plan the next year's IEP, parents should think about the progress their child has made over the past twelve months. Step back and observe your child's behavior, speech, and social skills. Be as objective as possible. If you feel she is progressing at the rate expected, you know the IEP is working. If she isn't progressing, the IEP needs to be revisited with changes made to help your child.

Further Education

At the age of fourteen, your child with autism reaches a transition stage. The first half of the transition is to determine what your child's goals will be. If your child is able to communicate his hopes for his future, his opinions should be part of the transition process. The second half addresses how the school will provide an education that will assist your child in meeting those goals.

DOES THIS SOUND LIKE YOUR CHILD?

School staff may say they are testing your child to determine her disability, but only a physician can diagnose a medical problem. Their documentation can only support the diagnosis. If you do not have an official diagnosis and intervention at school is being delayed, consult with a pediatric neurologist who is familiar with ASD.

Identifying Your Child's Interests

How do you determine the interests and talents that may be hidden in your child? If you don't have a computer at home, get one and load it with drawing, reading, and math software as well as other software of interest to children her age. Avoid the video game model where a child seems to be in a trance with repetitive activity; autism has enough of that without adding more. But games and activities that will stretch your child's mind are valuable.

You may discover that your child has a talent in graphic arts, or that math is second nature to her. You may find she knows more about computers than you do! Many people with autism are finding their way into technology fields because of the home computer. This is an especially strong field for people with Asperger's syndrome.

Another option to find the abilities that are within your child is applying the concept of "Take Your Child to Work" day. It doesn't have to be your place of employment; any activities you are involved in may be of interest to your child. He can garden with you, file movies and books away, help you paint a wall, or wash the car. Anything you do is something your child might be interested in, and it will give him more than just a window to watch the world through; it will also provide your child with a doorway to walk into the world.

The Traditional Educational Path

Some children with autism continue with traditional education throughout their school career. They may go on to college and become very successful at a chosen field. Being autistic does not preclude a college education and a career. Some people with autism have progressed to earn their doctorate and become a leader in their line of work.

DID YOU KNOW?

When your child turns fourteen, transition services must be included in the IEP. Watch for two things: the student's goals for his adult life and how the educational plan of the next year relates to those goals. Outside agencies involved with transition must attend the IEP as well.

There are two primary methods used to instruct children with autism: applied behavioral analysis (ABA) and Treatment and Education of Autistic and Related Communication Handicapped Children (TEACCH). There are supporters and detractors of each method; neither method is right or wrong, as what will work for one child may not be suitable for another child. Parents need to understand both methods and decide which is best for their child.

The TEACCH Method

TEACCH is the most commonly used method for the instruction of students with autism. Your school system may not use the term *TEACCH* for the structure they have in the classroom, but it is easily identified. It can be less intensive and therefore less stressful, especially for younger children.

The basis of TEACCH is visual learning and structure. The traits of autism are thus used to the instructor's advantage as well as to the student's benefit. Visualization is a powerful tool for people with autism and can be used in a child's learning. TEACCH uses schedules that are posted in various locations to help a child associate a picture with an activity; this helps with learning the usefulness of words as well as in creating a routine that can be relied on.

The ABA Method

ABA was developed from the principle of positive reinforcement techniques. Skills are taught to a child and when the skill is performed correctly, the child is rewarded, reinforcing the desired behavior, skill, or activity. Chapter 3 covers ABA therapy in more detail. Behaviors that are desirable for a child with autism to learn are taught at first, such as eye contact, imitative behavior, and language. When these skills have been mastered, they are used to build on, and then more complex skills are taught.

Parents' Expectations

If you can get through an entire school career without at least one major battle each year, you will have the respect and envy of every parent of a child with autism on the planet. Keeping your goals and expectations positive and realistic can minimize those battles, and if you have to engage in one, at least you know you can win. More importantly, your child can win.

There is a new PTA for you to join. Not the one at your child's school but the one that stands for

Parent   Teacher   Advocate

You are now all three in one package. You know you are a parent, and you may have figured out that you are your child's first and best teacher as well. You are also your child's best, and sometimes only, advocate. Running interference is just part of being a parent and it may be the first line appearing in your job description: parent of a child with autism.

Chapter 8

ASD and Adolescence

Ten Things You Will Learn in This Chapter

- What autism-related physical changes to expect during puberty
- The truth about seizures during adolescence
- The challenges of communication during the adolescent years
- Why you and your spouse must discuss your views on sexuality
- The details of informed consent
- How to prevent unwanted sexual advances
- When birth control may be helpful
- Systems for preparing your child for the changes of puberty
- Why a reliance on routine can be beneficial
- How to help your child recognize inappropriate behaviors

Physical Changes of Puberty

Puberty, teenager, adolescent. These are words a parent dreads, and it is no different for the parent of a child with autism. Many of the issues that arise during those years bring up questions and concerns that are difficult to solve. With the increase in autism, many affected children are now in their teens and people are beginning to collect information to make this time in a family's life easier. Teenage years can be fun and this is true for teens with autism as well.

Puberty is a time of changes, of testing the boundaries; it is a time of becoming mature, but acting immature; and it is a time of testing the world. For a child with autism it is all those things and more. Many changes happen to a child with autism when puberty arrives. Some are physical and others are emotional and mental.

Autism-Related Changes

If a child is prone to seizures, this time in his life will likely indicate the role seizures will play in his future. If he has not had seizures previously, he may begin them at puberty. If he already has them, they may increase or possibly cease. If your child's condition as related to seizures changes, consult with your physician. He or she may wish to make medication changes.

DID YOU KNOW?

The term *NT* or *neuro-typical* is used to refer to children who do not have autism. This avoids having to use the term *normal,* which is relative and which can suggest that being different is bad.

Another physical change can be related to bowel problems. A child who has had encopresis may suddenly be "cured." Bowel habits may become more regular and comfortable for your child. Be sure to discuss any concerns with your physician. If your child continues to have problems with bowel function, stool softeners can be most helpful.

Dealing with Other Changes

Most new issues you'll face when your child hits puberty are the same ones that any parent of a child in adolescence faces, but they can be harder to deal with if your child has autism. Acne is often an indicator of the hormonal changes in puberty, and it is difficult to get children to care for their skin. It is important, however, that this be done, as a child with severe skin eruptions is only that much more isolated from his peers. Establish a routine that keeps your child's skin clean and free of oil and bacteria; cleansing pads are good for this purpose.

Other physical changes are normal and natural but may confuse your child. Body hair begins to appear, boys' voices crack, girls develop breasts—your child wakes up in a new and unfamiliar body. If you find your child analyzing his or her body, ignore it. The novelty will go away and if you draw attention to it, you will inadvertently reinforce the behavior.

Emotional Changes of Puberty

Even more dramatic than the physical changes are the emotional and mental changes that a child experiences as he abandons childhood for adolescence. It is important for parents to fill in the gaps for their child to prevent further social isolation. Autism is isolating enough without puberty complicating the situation.

It is the job of the parents to be certain the things we assume our teenagers will do for themselves are still done. It is true that a child with autism may not be interested in the latest fashions at her school, but Mom and Dad need to be certain that their child is following sensible guidelines when choosing clothing. Your child may not care about the latest haircut or even whether she has taken a shower, but you need to care for her. A teenager's world turns on social acceptance and since children with autism struggle with social interaction, they need all of the help they can get.

Other emotional changes can include fragile emotions, willfulness, belligerence—your child may experience all of the emotions that any adolescent has when he enters puberty. If your child is inclined toward aggression or anger outbursts, do not be surprised if the nature of those outbursts changes. Some children have fewer outbursts while other children have more than they did before puberty. It is common for a child to have fewer but more intense outbursts.

Sexuality

It is difficult for parents when any child grows from the relative innocence of childhood to adulthood;

sexuality is a topic that requires education, explanation, and understanding. It can be bewildering and even frightening for a child. But when the child has autism, the problem is magnified. How does a person with autism express her sexuality when her social skills are challenged?

Mom and Dad, You Need to Talk

This is the most important thing you can do for your child. Both parents need to sit down together and talk about how they feel about puberty, adolescence, sexuality, and the role of sexuality for your children. It is important that you agree on issues of such importance. Individuals with autism have problems with sexuality that are as unique and diverse as they are; the only common thread is that all people on the autism spectrum have social issues that affect their behavior. The behaviors expressed vary like snowflakes; you will never see two alike.

Experiencing sexuality may not be appropriate for a child who has autism. Coming to terms with the fact that a child might not marry or have children someday is another loss for a parent struggling with the diagnosis of autism. When parents realize this part of their child's life may be diminished or nonexistent, it becomes another loss—another item on the list of things their child will not experience.

A BETTER PARENTING PRACTICE

Many adults are uncomfortable about dealing with the sexuality of their children. Parents need to put those feelings aside so that they can have a dialogue about this topic. If the conversation is delayed, you may find yourself facing an even more uncomfortable conversation after a bad situation arises that could have been prevented.

Some people with autism do not have a sexual drive at all, and if that is the case, there is no reason to try to change this. Some medications can cause a loss of libido; other times the cause is unknown. Given the problems a person with autism encounters with sexuality, a lack of sexual drive can be a blessing in disguise.

Understanding Sexuality

A person who is autistic and has a functioning libido will have difficulties expressing his or her sexuality in an appropriate manner. Matters of disease prevention, sexual abuse, birth control, and behavior management are difficult to explain to a young person, or an adult, who struggles with understanding concepts. As with the other things in your child's life that you have had to take control of, if his autism is severe enough to limit his judgment, you must take control of his sexuality as well. If it is any consolation, it will be harder on you as a parent than it will be on your child. No one wants to deny their child a life full of love and experiences, but sometimes it is the only choice available.

"Informed consent" between two adults is the generally accepted measure of whether a sexual activity is appropriate. Understanding what informed consent is will help you as a parent to assist your child as he grows up. Informed consent cannot happen unless an individual has several qualities:

- A person must be able to communicate to another person the word or the meaning of the word *no*.
- If a person is given different choices, she must demonstrate her ability to make a choice based on the information she has.
- A person must understand that there are appropriate places and times for sexual behavior.
- A person must be able to understand and detect danger and threats in order to react properly.
- A person must understand the word *no* and be able to cease an activity if told to do so.

There are many more factors involved in determining a person's ability to make an informed choice, but if these are not skills a child has, he is not capable of making sexual decisions for himself. And even if a child communicates well and clearly, social interactions may still be beyond his grasp. Saying "no" does a person little good if they don't know when to say it.

Unwanted Sexual Advances
Primarily parents need to consider the risk factors as they make decisions. HIV/AIDS is a risk for

any kind of unprotected sexual contact that involves bodily fluids. Children with autism are also easy targets for sexual abuse, as they do not always understand dangerous, threatening, or inappropriate situations. Parents should not let themselves be ruled by fear, but they need to become proactive in the protection of their children.

Children and adults with autism have every right to have friendships and relationships. If parents are in charge of their child's sexuality, their goal should be to help the child understand her sexuality as much as possible to prevent their child from becoming a victim of unwanted sexual activity.

When a child has a sexual experience against his will, or without his understanding, it is very hard on the entire family. Preventing sexual activity through behavior modification is the ideal method for families to choose before a problem occurs.

Menstruation

Since 75 percent of children with autism are boys, there is not a lot of information available for dealing with menstruation in girls with autism. Considering what a monumental step this is for any girl, it can be frightening for a girl who has communication deficits. It may be natural, but it is still blood, and it is alarming. It is reassuring to know that few girls with autism are unable to learn how to deal with their periods, and although the transition can be difficult, it can be done.

Indications of Menarche

The best way to deal with a girl beginning her menstrual cycle is to be prepared for it ahead of time. Watching for the signs that show parents a young girl is entering into menarche will allow you to prepare and teach your daughter. You will be able to observe discreetly, and when you know that it is imminent, you can begin preparing your daughter for this new stage of her life.

When girls enter puberty, their behavior may be the first indication. In most children, this is obvious. Parents, particularly dads, will notice the irritability in their daughter; things that were once loved by her are now a source of embarrassment. It takes little to provoke a bad mood in a prepubescent girl and anger outbursts are common as well. But how do you recognize the arrival of puberty when irritability and outbursts are part of the daily routine?

DOES THIS SOUND LIKE YOUR CHILD?

Children with autism are notoriously immodest. If you permitted your children to run around without clothing when they were young, puberty is the time to teach them modesty. Children with autism do not understand that different environments require different clothing, and you don't want your teen stripping in the grocery store.

It is important for parents to be attuned with their daughter's behavior. Routines can now be your best friend; even though you may feel a slave to them, use them to be aware of what is going on with your daughter. If things are upsetting her that didn't six or twelve months ago, and you see a hair-trigger temper, that is a warning sign for you.

Breast development is usually the first physical sign that puberty has arrived. Her figure will start changing; she will develop hips and a waistline. She may develop quickly or slowly, as each girl is individual in her growth. These are changes she may or may not acknowledge; it entirely depends on how aware of her own body she is. At this point, it is time to start preparing her for the start of her menstrual cycle. The rule of thumb is that within one year of the development of breasts, her period will begin.

Preparing Your Daughter

Visualization is your primary tool in teaching about menstruation. Begin a role-playing project that will mimic what happens during your daughter's period. Buy an easy-to-read calendar and put it in the bathroom. Purchase supplies and select several different brands for your daughter to see. She may have a sensory reaction to one product and prefer another one based on criteria that do not apply to you. The color of the package, the shape of the pad, or an odor associated with the packaging will be some of her determining variables.

Begin by showing your daughter the calendar and the pads. Talk to her as though she understands each word you say even if she is totally nonverbal. Take a red pen, circle the date on the calendar, and then place some red food coloring on the pad. The goal is to imitate in a nonthreatening way what she will see when her periods begin. Handle the situation in a matter-of-fact manner. Dispose of the "used" pad, replace it in her clothing, and repeat this every two to three hours. Continue this practice for about five days. Twenty-eight days later, repeat the process.

Theory into Practice

When you begin teaching your daughter how to handle the hygiene issues of having a period, it is important that a woman be part of the instructional process. If you are a single dad, you need to find some help. A girl should never believe that it is appropriate and acceptable for any male, of any age or relationship to her, to be in any kind of intimate contact with her. That is a rule that can never be broken. Single fathers can rely on their own mother, sister, a school nurse, or another trusted female. It is impossible to teach a girl what is appropriate for her own body if that rule is not adhered to closely.

DID YOU KNOW?

If the menstrual cycle is extremely difficult and hygiene is a constant battle, discuss your options with your daughter's doctor. Some physicians put girls with autism on medication to suppress their periods. This may be an option if medically appropriate.

When the big day arrives, and remember, you will have no warning of the actual date, fall back on your planning techniques. Take it in stride as you circle the day on the calendar and attend to hygiene. Remember to teach her proper disposal of the pads and be sure you keep a supply of her preferred brand.

There are no guarantees this will be the magic bullet and that your daughter's periods will begin and continue uneventfully. There are likely to be trying times for the entire family. Hygiene may be a continual problem or it may go smoothly, without any problems at all. Every child is different and there is no way to know how she will feel about any of this. If you can convey calmness and avoid a production over the situation, the chances are greater she will take it in stride.

Birth Control
It is easier for parents to make decisions regarding their child's sexuality if they proceed with a philosophy of discretion being the better part of valor. Sexuality is always a matter of informed consent between two adults. Factoring in the mental age of your child and his or her social abilities is essential. Unfortunately, no policy can exclude the possibility of sexual conduct that is unplanned, and for girls on the autism spectrum, this is a problem.

Most states do not allow permanent methods of birth control to be used on a child, even if he or she is over the age of majority. There are no exceptions to those laws for children with disabilities. If your child is impaired enough that having children is out of the question, check with the laws in your state to find out what can and cannot be done.

So how do parents prevent an unplanned pregnancy that is the result of their child engaging in sexual contact without understanding the implications of the activity? Many physicians will prescribe a birth control method for girls with autism or other spectrum disorders that can be taken daily in a pill form, injected every few weeks (frequency depending on the patient), or implanted. The advantage to the injections or implants is that the concern is removed without the daily use of a pill. The disadvantage can be the possible side effects of these methods of birth control, including weight gain, headaches, and problems that may be associated with long-term use of these medications.

It may be unfair that parents of boys with autism do not have as much to be concerned about in this area, but the reality is that girls are at a much higher risk for the consequences of sexual activity. It is not important, at this point, to make a point regarding the responsibility of sexual behavior; the important issue is to protect your daughter.

Inappropriate Behaviors

Although there are many behaviors that can be considered inappropriate, none upset people quite like those behaviors that are sexual in nature. Because of inappropriate behaviors, the deficit in social skills is even more evident and isolating for the person with autism. Children become aware at very young ages that it is inappropriate to touch other people in certain places;

a child with autism does not have that built-in control and may reach out to touch a body part of someone out of curiosity. This is particularly common in adolescent boys attempting to touch a woman's breast. Dealing with these behaviors when a child is young is important so that they are not a problem when a child becomes an adult.

Self-Stimulating Behaviors

This is a difficult subject for parents. When they discover their child with autism actively masturbating with not the least hint of discretion, they wonder how to handle the situation. To keep a proper perspective on this activity, remember that all children masturbate. NT children just aren't caught doing it. Children with autism have no inhibitions, because they are unaware of the social taboo against masturbating in public.

A BETTER PARENTING PRACTICE

If your child engages in self-stimulating behavior excessively, genital irritation can result. A quick (and very discreet) check when your child showers will let you know if this is a problem. Some medications used for autism, notably SSRIs, will also slow down the libido and may be appropriate if this behavior is out of control; your physician can best advise you on this.

The mistake that parents will often make—and it is an easy one to make—is when they find their child masturbating in a public area. Their goal is to stop the behavior immediately, and they will usually shout or sharply pull their child's hand away. That does stop the behavior, but it also sends a message that sexuality and the human body are bad or dirty.

Your goal should not be to stop the behavior, but rather to redirect it to an appropriate time and location. Masturbating in the middle of the living room is not appropriate, and redirecting your child to his or her bedroom (with a closed door) will solve most of those public displays. Keep in mind that people with autism are dictated by the structure of their routine. If they are taught that their bedroom is the only acceptable location for self-stimulating behavior, they will adhere to that routine.

Inappropriate Touching of Others

The majority of paraprofessionals that work with students with autism are female. Females are also still in a majority as caregivers, whether it be at home, day care, or in other environments that care for children. A young boy with autism who has raging hormones in his system may not understand that touching others in a sexual manner is not acceptable.

This behavior is not malicious or intended to degrade. Your child has no idea that it is unacceptable to touch another person inappropriately. The behavior must be stopped. It may be somewhat humorous when a ten-year-old child does it, but if it's allowed to continue, it will not be nearly so funny when he is a thirty-year-old man.

Generally, the situation will resolve itself. A girl is less inclined to engage in this behavior. And when a boy crosses the line, a woman's natural reaction when touched inappropriately will generally solve the problem; most males do not enjoy a slap across the face. The most important thing that parents and school personnel can do is teach your child that this is not allowed in any circumstances so that the behavior is not a problem when the child is too big to redirect him. It is much easier to modify behaviors in a child than it is to change those same behaviors in an adult.

Teaching your children about inappropriate sexual behavior is difficult because obviously you are not going to demonstrate. There are books for very young children that have drawings geared toward children who might not understand the language, which might be helpful. The goal is to help your child with autism learn to control his sexual behavior in a way that will keep him safe.

Chapter 9

What Will Adult Life Be Like for Your Child?

Ten Things You Will Learn in This Chapter

- Which daily activities are important preparations for independence
- How to create a routine for activities of daily living
- The importance of providing an interesting environment to an adult with autism
- How modern-day institutions are not the fortresses of the past
- The benefits of group homes and assisted living
- The best options for adults with high-functioning autism
- How buying a home now can help your child as an adult
- Why having a will doesn't replace the need for a trust fund
- How to choose a trustee
- Why life insurance is something to think about now

Living Independently

When people have children, they have expectations and goals for their life and their children's lives. One of those goals is watching a child grow to independence. Parents are truly satisfied when they know their adult child is equipped to face and handle the world. But having a child with autism forces parents to re-evaluate that goal and determine what the future will be as their child becomes an adult.

In a perfect world, children with autism would mature and acquire enough skills to live on their own. They would understand the things that are needed to live safely on their own: balancing checkbooks, turning off stoves, locking doors, and handling all the daily activities to which most people never give a second thought.

But before the bigger issues of independent living can be addressed, parents and caretakers must be sure that a young adult with autism can be responsible for his own personal care and hygiene. A young adult must be able to

- Bathe or shower daily
- Independently use the bathroom
- Use deodorant, skin care products, and other toiletries appropriately
- Brush and floss his teeth
- Brush his hair
- Dress properly for weather conditions
- Dress appropriately for work, leisure, and sleep
- Determine which clothes need to be laundered
- Take medications at the proper times in the proper dosages

Most children with autism do learn all of these things and develop a routine from which they seldom depart. If you have a child who is six years old and he has not mastered all of these skills, don't worry. He may be behind but the odds are very good that he will catch up and have his own system to care for himself. Parents sometimes forget that children who are not autistic resist brushing their teeth and washing their hands, so it isn't always autism that is the culprit. Sometimes it is just being a kid.

Building Daily Care Habits

As parents work with a child to build the habits and skills she will need as an adult, they learn that the trait of living by a routine can work in their favor. If your child heavily relies on a routine to make sense of her world, use that to teach her the skills she needs.

Making Lists

Before you begin building a routine to teach activities of daily living (ADLs), sit down with a piece of paper and pencil and outline all of the skills that are necessary for your child. All people have some common activities, such as bathing and using the bathroom, but there are many individual ones as well. Some children need to use certain skin care products to treat acne or eczema as well.

Make a list and divide it into three parts: morning, afternoon, and evening. In your three-part schedule, list out the activities that occur, or should occur, during those times. For instance, the morning list might include using the bathroom, brushing teeth, showering, medications, and so forth. Do this for all three sections, listing out all the activities you can think of. Keep the list handy for a few days and add in the things you overlooked so the list will be as complete as possible.

Creating a Communication Board

Now you can start teaching your child to make this list second nature. If your child is nonverbal, make a communication panel and put it in the bathroom where he will be able to reference it easily. Attaching small drawings that represent the activity are good or you can use photographs (keeping in mind your child's privacy). Attach them with Velcro so you can adjust the order in which things are done if necessary.

The next step is simple. Start the routine each morning with your child. Explain to her as you go through it what she is to do and point to the picture on the communication board. If she is verbal, a cheat-sheet on the wall that she can read is another option. After three to four weeks, a new routine will have developed. Keep an eye on it until you are confident that she has mastered the skills. That is one less thing for you to worry about as your child learns to get herself ready each morning!

Repeat this entire procedure for the afternoon and evening care. The most important part is following the schedule closely. Be certain your child follows it as well. As mentioned before, people with autism are ruled by their routine, and this self-care routine will be something that will help your child achieve independence.

A BETTER PARENTING PRACTICE

An instant camera can make quick work of creating visual cues that help your child understand his life and routine. Take photos of his tooth brush, the bathtub, his clothes, and other items he uses. This will make your communication panel unique and specific to his needs.

Residential Living

Many parents have their children live at home after they reach adulthood. However, this is not always the best choice for an adult child or for the parents. There are other available options and there are no blanket answers as to the best solution for a given child. It isn't just the child's abilities that determine what is best for the family. It is also the family's needs, lifestyle, available emotional and physical resources, and finances.

Remaining at Home

This is one of the biggest topics discussed in support groups across the country. Someone will usually, and tentatively, ask the question, "What do I do when my child is grown?" The most important consideration in deciding where your child will live as an adult should be whether or not the environment is productive and interesting. Whether your child lives at home with you, lives in a group home, or needs to be institutionalized, the life she leads must be actively in touch with the world around her. As a child turns into a young adult, and then from a young adult into a mature adult, his happiness and satisfaction will hinge on his environment.

One of the most distinctive aspects of autism makes it imperative that an adult with autism has an environment full of variety and interest. It is too easy for many people with autism to retreat into their own world and if that is allowed to continue, they can retreat further and further from those around them. Couple that with the lack of conceptual understanding, and it is easy to see how someone with autism becomes a couch potato, staring at a television for hours on end.

If you wish to keep your adult child at home with you, be sure you have the physical and mental capacity to keep him busy. He will need to participate in various activities, have a schedule that keeps him interested (and whatever you do, stick to the schedule as much as possible), and he will need to be physically active. You will need to either keep up with that schedule yourself or have someone in the home that can. You will also need to plan ahead to make arrangements for someone to care for your child when age and health make it impossible for you to do so.

Group Homes

Group homes and assisted living are the options most parents choose for their children on the autism spectrum. Group homes are generally staffed with four to six residents. Two staff members are on the schedule at all times except during sleeping hours, when one is sufficient, and other personnel for special therapies come in and out. These homes are usually single-family residences in neighborhoods around the country.

Group homes are very popular for several reasons:

- People with autism see people without disabilities and thus have role models outside their immediate family members.
- People in the community are exposed to autism and learn they are people like anyone else.
- Group homes with several people give everyone a chance to continue a degree of socialization.
- Therapies and education are provided to the residents in group homes and life skills are taught by staff members or other qualified people.
- Activities are planned regularly such as swimming, bowling, and field trips that everyone enjoys.
- Group homes may be permanent but they can also teach a young adult with autism the skills necessary to live independently or return home to live with parents and other family members.

Assisted living is for people with high-functioning autism who need less supervision than those in a group home. Two people may share living arrangements and have a social services worker visit daily to be sure that their needs are being met. Each of these situations would vary depending on the people involved and their abilities.

Institutionalized Living

When you think of institutions, you may think of the horror stories that you've heard rumors about or seen in films. It is true that institutions in the past were the last stop for people with mental disabilities. It is also true that abuse and neglect were common problems for the people unfortunate enough to find themselves placed in an institution. Much of the problem came from a lack of understanding of the various disabilities and illnesses that affected people. The social isolation of an institution only added to the situation, as no one in a community really knew what was going on behind the closed doors.

Institutions in the modern era can be modern and have a homelike setting. They can be clean without looking like a hospital and be geared toward meeting the needs of the residents. Professionals who enjoy working with the mentally challenged population staff them. It is possible and those facilities do exist.

DID YOU KNOW?

The important thing to know is that no parent, whether she chooses an institution, group or assisted-living, or keeps her adult child at home, is wrong in her decision. Don't let pressure from family, friends, or society make you feel bad for your decision.

An institution is something that may be appropriate for a person with autism if he has behavioral disorders that can be a source of danger to himself or others. Group homes or assisted-living facilities do not have the close supervision that may be necessary for such a patient. An institution may be suitable also for patients who have physical complications requiring a great deal of therapy and/or medications.

Providing after You Are Gone

If you do not have a will, put down this book and call an attorney to have one drawn up immediately. After you have an appointment, begin reading again and make some notes about what pertains to you and your family. The worst thing that could possibly happen is for something to happen to you or your spouse when you have no provisions made for your child. Everyone asks what the worst-case scenario is when you have a child with autism: The death of parents who have not prepared for their child is the worst-case scenario.

Asset Protection

When a young couple marries and begins to build a life, they make plans for the future. Seldom do they think that the decisions they make in their twenties may affect their baby when he is a senior citizen. But it is important for parents of a child with autism to protect all of their assets to provide for their child when he is an adult.

In our highly mobile society, the average family moves at least every seven years. Many families move more often. Most of these families own a home and as the years go by; they sell, buy, and upgrade a little each time. They start with a small home, move to a moderately sized one, and have the goal of a certain kind of house that will be their last home purchase. As a result, there is no "family home" and no mortgage ever gets paid in full.

A BETTER PARENTING PRACTICE

Although many states have made it legal for a person to write his or her own will, it is not advisable for the parent of a child with a disability to do so. If a parent has made his or her own will, it is more vulnerable to being successfully contested. Get the assistance of a licensed attorney.

If you have not yet bought a home, it would be wise to start working toward that goal. If you can stay in that house, perhaps improving or remodeling it, your house value will increase, your mortgage payments will be stable, and it will be paid in full in fifteen to thirty years. That is the most valuable asset your child could ever have. Although he would need someone to handle his finances, that house you are considering buying now, or may already own, will provide him with security for his entire life.

Cars, jewelry, paintings, stocks and bonds, and just about every other asset you have can go down in value. A house, on land that you own, is valuable security not only for you and your family now, but also in the distant future for your child with autism.

Trust Funds

A trust fund is often set up by a parent to provide for a child's needs. Because a child with autism is not likely to understand money management when she is an adult, preparations to protect her future are important. Although a will does declare where you wish your assets to go, a trust fund has funds and assets that can be distributed over a person's lifetime. As with guardianship, it is important to select a trusted friend or organization to oversee the trust fund. It is possible to select more than one trustee if you wish to have the responsibility shared.

Every state has different laws governing how trusts are set up and maintained, and it is important that you are aware of your state's regulations. Most states have two types of trust funds, one of which is of particular interest to the parents of a disabled child. An after-death trust can be set up to protect the financial needs of a child when both parents are deceased. An estate attorney can best advise you concerning your specific needs, concerns, and state laws.

DID YOU KNOW?

When you appoint in your will someone to care for your child's finances, be absolutely certain of your confidence and trust in this person. It might be wise to consider a professional accountant, who is subject to audits, to protect your child's interests.

The trustee, or person(s) you appoint to oversee the trust, must be someone you trust implicitly. Trustees are held to a high accountability, both legally and morally, and although they may be paid a small fee for their services, the judgment they provide is beyond value. If you chose a family member or friend, be certain they understand financial management. If they can be trusted to fulfill your wishes and your child's needs, but lack some knowledge in the finer points of money, don't hesitate to also appoint an accountant or other professional to advise your primary trustee.

Guardians

If something happens to you or your spouse, do you know who will take care of your children—especially your child with autism? Most people feel confident that a family member would step in, but when a crisis such as this happens, it doesn't always work out that smoothly.

In choosing potential guardians, make a list of the people you feel would be the best to raise your child in the event you are unable to. Then talk to those people in a setting where you have their total attention and it isn't an "off the cuff" conversation. This is a serious decision for all parties concerned. Outline what your child's needs are now and what those needs are apt to be in the future. Explain what financial resources would be available, what health issues your child has, and what you would want done in his adult years.

As you compile this list of people, think about your child, his life, and the lives of the people you are considering asking. If it is a family member, perhaps your own brother or sister, does he or she have a career that might make this responsibility difficult? Also, consider the person's lifestyle and how he feels about his family life. One person who has eight children might easily handle another one, even one with autism, but another person with a large family might panic at the idea of one more child.

When you approach people about assuming care of your child, they may have several reactions. One possibility is that they would want, or insist, on caring for your child. Another reaction is that they need to think it through and consider different options, and yet another reaction may be that they know this would not be the right decision for them or their family. There is no right or wrong answer in this.

A BETTER PARENTING PRACTICE

You may hope that your other children would step in to care for your child with autism if the need arose. But the older siblings of a child with autism may or may not feel up to this. Making a will with a sibling as the first choice and having four or five alternatives leaves everyone's options open.

When you have a list of people who would be willing to step in, have your will state those people by name as your choice to raise your children. It is wise to have several names in case something prevents one of them from stepping in. If you have more than one name on the list in your will, you can avoid having to rewrite your will every six months, and it will save attorney's fees. It will also give you peace of mind to know that you have done all you can to protect your child and his interests.

Financial Protection

Every family attempts to protect itself financially, but when there is a child with autism involved, this protection becomes much more critical. Mom and Dad find they are making decisions that affect the "here and now," as well as the distant future.

Insurance

One of the smartest investments a couple can make when they have children, especially if a child is disabled, is to purchase life insurance—a lot of life insurance—as much as you can afford to buy. When you are young and healthy, the rates are much lower than if you wait until your late thirties or forties to purchase a policy.

IRAs and Other Funds

Parents can, through their employer, set up various financial plans that will protect and increase their money over the years. IRAs and other retirement plans can protect a family in many different ways. Tax benefits can be seen immediately, and funds will be available to provide for family members upon retirement or in the case of an unexpected death. IRAs supersede the will, so be certain you keep your beneficiary updated.

Every state differs in regulations regarding financial matters. Financial planning is a complex subject with many pitfalls for the uninformed. If you are planning to set up a portfolio for your family's security, consult with an accountant and estate planning attorney for the best course of action. You will be preparing not just for your lifetime, but for your child's lifetime as well.

Chapter 10

Assistive Techniques and Technologies

Ten Things You Will Learn in This Chapter

- When assistive devices are right for your child
- How computers can suit your child's visual mind
- The possibilities of a touch-screen monitor
- How to ease the challenge of typing
- Why a wireless computer mouse may not be helpful
- Which computer programs can best help your child
- The use of guide animals for children with autism
- The right age to bring a guide dog into your home
- How to build your own assistive devices at home
- When sidewalk chalk and a photo album are what you need

Computers as Aids

Any device or item that can help a person with autism compensate for his or her deficits is considered assistive. There are many forms of assistive devices—some are based on sophisticated technology and others are very basic and can be made at home. Others are not devices at all but are living, breathing animals that are "on the job" when their services are needed. Anything you use or adapt that helps your child function to the best of his or her ability is an assistive device.

Children with autism seem to have a natural flair for computers. It takes little time for them to understand how the computer operates. Their abilities on the computer are amazing; a child may be nonverbal and restricted by his own repetitive activities, but put that child in front of a computer and you are the one limited, not him. Children with autism have the ability to understand computers better than they understand other human beings. Understanding how an autistic person's mind works, and how computers work, helps people without autism understand why this is and what it could mean for a child.

Visual "Thinking"

Visualization is a very helpful tool for people with autism. The autistic mind processes things visually, so it is the strongest learning center a person with autism has. Think of the mind and its functions as being similar to a series of snapshots. Each photograph represents a memory or an understanding of something specific.

The brain of a person with autism stores memories and knowledge in that format. One snapshot or picture of something tells them what they need to know.

DOES THIS SOUND LIKE YOUR CHILD?

If your child engages in self-stimulating and obsessive repetitive behaviors, consider getting him his own computer. This does not have to be a top-of-the-line model. A basic computer on which you can install programs and run CDs is enough. The unacceptable behaviors will likely be reduced, and he will be learning simultaneously.

Visual thinking is a nonlinear style of thinking. It is associative, and the memories and knowledge of a person with ASD are not filed in the brain the same way that they are in a person without autism.

Computers also "think" in that manner. Each file or "memory" can be brought up on the screen, intact and self-contained. If you can access that file, you can access everything you need to know about that memory. And carrying this a step further, associative links, tying together different parts of the computer, create the complete memory. Therefore, seemingly unrelated memories are linked together to make a whole picture. The computer sees the link and understands why, even if the typical person does not.

A person with autism thinks in a similar manner, and what seems like techno-babble is in fact a logically ordered visual system used by both the autistic mind and the computer. Computers and people with autism think alike.

Daily Life with the Computer

Many people reserve the use of the home computer as a reward for children who have successfully completed their chores or homework. It is viewed as a recreational item, and like any privilege, it can be removed. But for a child with autism, a computer is an important part of everyday life and not just a privilege; it is a communication tool, learning aid, and social companion.

Children who have autism have realized many benefits from their use of computers. With computers, attention, motivation, and organizational skills have increased in children with autism, as has the ability to independently handle skills for self-help. Socialization has also improved, and expressive language becomes more appropriate and useful for a child with autism. The computer has helped to organize and bring order to your child's disordered world.

Helpful Accessories

Various accessories to the computer have helped children with autism learn various programs, games, and activities. For children with deficits in fine motor skills, some of these devices can make the computer easier to use. Other devices can help a child who struggles with the understanding of concepts, bridging the gap between the abstract and the concrete.

Monitor Devices

One of the most popular assistive devices on the market is the touch screen window, which limits or eliminates the need to use the mouse. Schools and libraries often have a touch screen window because it reduces the risk of a mouse being lost or stolen, so if your child is older, she may have already used this device.

DID YOU KNOW?

A QWERTY keyboard has the keys placed in the accustomed arrangement (the first letters in the top row spell out *QWERTY*). ABC keyboards are also available, which may or may not be suitable for your child. The QWERTY is not at all difficult for a child to learn and it will become second nature for your child to use one.

A touch screen provides a major benefit to children who have a conceptual problem understanding that the mouse controls movement on the screen. When a child can become involved "with" the computer, he will derive more benefit from its possibilities. Removing the mouse for a child that struggles with this issue will reduce frustration and the subsequent behaviors that may occur.

If your child has problems with overstimulation when she uses the computer, it could be caused by the glare from the computer. Some people are ultrasensitive to the light of a computer monitor, which will cause fatigue, eyestrain, and headaches. Many inexpensive filters are available that can be placed over the screen to reduce the glare and make the time on the computer less fatiguing. This will also ease overstimulation, if that is a concern.

Keyboard Devices

Some children with autism have problems with fine motor skills and have limited dexterity. An alternative keyboard can ease the problems encountered when attempting to type on the small standard-sized keys. This is also good for preschool children who are learning hand-eye coordination.

When shopping for alternative keyboards, remember that you won't be able to find every feature on one keyboard. You need to prioritize your child's needs and then make a decision. If he has problems with dexterity, a keyboard with large keys would be helpful. If he has vision problems, a lighted keyboard would help. There are many sizes and shapes of keyboards; comparing what is available will help you make the best choice.

A BETTER PARENTING PRACTICE

When choosing the peripheral equipment for your child's computer, cross off *wireless mouse* from your shopping list. There are few things more upsetting than an enraged child with autism who can't find his computer mouse. A corded mouse is also difficult to throw in an anger outburst.

After the computer is set up, if your child has some problems with the operation of the keyboard, check in the operating system for accessibility options. You can program the keyboard to specialized function—for example, ignore rapidly repeating strokes if your child tends to rest his hands directly on the keys. Several options can personalize the computer and make it easier to operate.

Mouse Devices

The computer you bought came with a mouse that was the most basic mouse available. It left-clicks, right-clicks, and moves the cursor. It is small and probably not very efficient. Other options may work better for your child.

Trackball mice are very popular, and with good reason. The mouse is stationary, solid, and versatile. The ball is in a fixed position within the mouse and is operated by either fingers or thumb. Left- and right-handed versions are available. The trackball is easy to get used to and will give your child more control of her activities on the computer.

Useful Software

Once your child's computer is set up, it is time to load it with programs and software.

Look for programs that are educational but are also fun. No one can expect any child to stick with a program if it is boring. Math programs based on popular cartoon characters are a great favorite and illustrate clearly the concepts necessary to understand the skills being taught in the program. Instead of just hearing that one plus one equals two, a computer program can show it. This will be helpful to the primary learning method of your child—the more visual the program, the better it will work for him.

Programs created for the child with ASD will be extremely useful but a little more difficult to find. Buying these programs on the Internet is the most convenient. These programs can address the problems children on the autism spectrum face regularly; speech (receptive and expressive), dexterity, and social interaction are some of the areas these programs address.

Service Dogs

The use of service dogs for assistance is a relatively new concept for people with autism. A service dog can reduce the risk of elopement, aid in socialization, and protect children with ASD in a public environment.

Before you get so enthusiastic that you run down to the local dog adoption center, several things must be considered. Any time an animal is brought into your home, whether it is trained by an agency or you self-train, it is a decision that must carefully be weighed. Remember that a service dog is there to work, and work he will; whenever your child and her service dog are together, the dog is working. But a dog is still a dog; it has to be allowed to play, dig holes, torment the family cat, and do all the things dogs do. Your success will be determined by how well you integrate the needs of the child and the needs of the dog.

It is vitally important that a child not be frightened of large dogs before you get a service dog. If your child is very young and you are considering this option for the future, expose your child to larger dogs that you know are comfortable with children. It can be alarming for a child who has never been around a large dog to suddenly have an animal at eye level. A hesitant or scared child will not bond with the dog, and no training in the world will allow them to perform as a good team.

DID YOU KNOW?

The Department of Justice states that animals other than dogs may be used as a service animal. Cats, ferrets, and parrots are very helpful service animals with a child who has autism. Determining what your goal is will help you determine which animal is appropriate for your child.

One parent must be involved in the dog/child team. If there are many caretakers involved, this will be confusing for both the child and the dog. One adult who can supervise the team and provide the dog with direction as to what is expected at a given moment will help the dog perform to the best of its ability. Children best adapt to a service dog after they become toddlers and before they enter school for the first time. A rule of thumb is ages two or three to six, with exceptions, of course—a child this age will be more receptive to the concept of dog/child teamwork.

Homemade Assistive Devices

You do not need a technological piece of equipment to provide an assistive device to your child. Many of the most efficient items are readily available at any variety store. If you think of a step stool as an assistive device for someone not tall enough to reach the top of the refrigerator, it is easy to understand how many things can be used to help your child compensate.

Next time you visit your local variety or office supply store, take a shopping cart and load it with things you think could be useful in helping your child. Some ideas to get you started are provided, but use your imagination:

- Dry erase boards, either formatted for scheduling or blank, or possibly both
- Inexpensive photo albums
- Notebook rings that are loose in the package
- Plastic storage bins of varying sizes
- Sidewalk chalk in various colors
- Yarn or string
- Magnetic letters and numbers
- Personalized pens and pencils with your child's name on them
- A laminator

Consider your child's strengths and weaknesses and be a little creative in coming up with solutions. For example, small storage bins could hold laminated cards that show an activity or chore that has to be done. This would help a child who does not sequence daily activities well. As your child completes each activity—such as brushing his teeth—he can move the card to the "Job Completed" bin. This will assist with sequencing and will provide motivation because the task completion is easily seen.

Sidewalk chalk can be used to provide direction if a child tends to wander when she goes outside with you; it can also show the limits of an area she is allowed to explore. Personalized writing tools are a great way to teach ownership; if your child uses the entire family's belongings, having his name on things will help him understand what is his and what isn't. Magnetic letters and numbers can be used in many ways—to mark a special occasion or holiday or to put up a goal for the day. You are limited only by your imagination.

Chapter 11

Financial Assistance and Emotional Support

Ten Things You Will Learn in This Chapter

- Social Security's definition of autism
- How the Wechsler Adult Intelligence Scale works
- Why specific language on evaluations is what you want
- The keys to navigating SSI and the SSA
- How to determine what *functioning* means
- How to file paperwork to apply for SSI
- Where to find federal assistance in your state
- Why it's important to know your insurance policy
- When respite care might be necessary
- How to find a respite worker to help your family

Social Security Benefits

Autism can be an expensive and emotionally taxing condition to deal with. Having good medical coverage and a supportive family are important, but those aren't always easy to come by. Fortunately, there are some ways to get help.

Autism is a "pervasive developmental disorder characterized by social and significant communication deficits originating prior to age 22." It seems hard for many to define autism in just a few words, but the Social Security Administration (SSA) has figured out how to sum it up neatly. They define mental retardation as a "significantly subaverage general intellectual functioning with deficits in adaptive behavior usually manifested before age 22." When a family seeks out disability benefits for their child, they will first turn to Social Security. As it is the baseline for the determination of a disability, it is important to understand how the SSA operates to determine if a child is disabled.

Educational and financial decisions are based on the results of IQ testing on children with autism. This is a very controversial area with parents, as there are concerns about the reliability of an IQ test on a child who has communication deficits.

The Wechsler Adult Intelligence Scale (WAIS) is the primary test that is used by the SSA to determine if a person is mentally retarded. A psychologist or psychiatrist must give the test and interpret the results. The same person must also write an evaluation to the SSA stating that the test was valid and accurately reflected the mental status of the individual who was tested. Three areas are tested: verbal, performance, and IQ. The SSA uses the lowest of the three assessments to determine a person's eligibility for benefits. But it is not only the score of the WAIS that factors into this decision; it is also how this score compares to the rest of the population.

DOES THIS SOUND LIKE YOUR CHILD?

Do not be alarmed if IQ testing is required for your child. The IQ score can be helpful in determining what assistance your child needs and can direct you in making medical and educational decisions; if you believe it is not truly reflective of your child's intelligence, that is fine. IQ will likely fluctuate over the years while your child hones her communication skills.

If a child is unable to be evaluated by the WAIS, other tests can be used. The Raven Progressive Matrices is for people with limited verbal ability and can be helpful for people with autism. The Minnesota Multiphasic Personality Inventory (MMPI) and the Thematic Apperception Test (TAT) are often useful if a child has other brain disorders and can help with supporting those diagnoses.

Supplemental Security Income

If you meet income and asset requirements, your child with autism may qualify for disability support through Social Security. There was a time that a diagnosis of autism meant an automatic allowance for Supplemental Security Income (SSI), but changes at the Social Security Administration (SSA) have made it so there is no guarantee that a child with autism will receive SSI payments. A simple diagnosis is no longer enough—parents must prove that their child cannot function "normally" in society in order to be eligible.

Function, Function, Function

Social functioning is a person's ability to relate to and with others. Adults and children have different social skills, but if a person is unable to maneuver through his social environment, he will have difficulty interacting with others in an educational or vocational environment.

Function is a relative term. If you ask one person how your child functions, he or she may see an entirely different picture than you do. A physician will see function in one way, and it will be entirely different than how a teacher sees it. This can be frustrating for parents, because they see the whole picture and understand exactly what the differences are in people's perceptions of their child. The problem enters in when a disability examiner, who has never met your child and likely never will, attempts to judge and decide how much of a deficit exists in your child's functioning.

If you remember how the disability examiner is looking at the decision he or she will have to make, it is easier to understand what information will help them reach the correct conclusion. According to Social Security, a child must have a "marked and severe functional limitation," or he is not disabled. The operative word here is *and*. It must be both marked and severe, so it is up to the people writing reports and records to show if this is the case. Another phrase that can be an issue is the requirement that a child must have "qualitative deficits in verbal and nonverbal communication and in imaginative activity," and again the key word is the same.

A BETTER PARENTING PRACTICE

Do not allow vague phrases on reports. If someone says your child is doing well and what he or she means is that there hasn't been a meltdown in a week, it could be interpreted to mean that it is no longer a severe disability. Ask teachers, doctors, and anyone else who evaluates your child to be as specific as possible.

Try to view your child as someone would who has never seen her before. Does her autism restrict her from activities that NT children of the same age participate in? Does she have communication problems severe enough that she has difficulty expressing what she needs to anyone outside of the family? Does she lack a sense of danger? Is she unable to care for herself in a socially appropriate manner? If your answers are "yes," it is your job as your child's advocate to see that this information is conveyed to Social Security effectively and accurately.

Presenting an Accurate Picture

Knowing how the severity of your child's disability will be determined is the most important piece of information you have. Medical sources, as well as educational and social sources, can be used to support your claim that your child is disabled. This includes reports on how he lives his daily life: how he functions with others, his attention span, obsessive behaviors, tantrums, aggression, and other issues in his life that interfere with typical functioning. Reports can be submitted from any source you deem appropriate. These statements can be from immediate or extended family members, day care staff, community service workers, respite care workers, or any other person involved with your child on a regular basis.

How to Apply for SSI

Applying for benefits is not difficult but it is a tedious and time-consuming process. The best way to proceed is to organize your financial records and all of the medical documentation you have so that it is at hand when you begin the application.

1. Gather all your documentation in advance: a certified copy of your child's birth certificate, tax and earnings records, name and address of medical and educational providers, and contact information for anyone who sees your child regularly.

2. Call Social Security at 1-800-772-1213, or go into a local office if there is one in your area, and request forms for the application of Childhood Disability Benefits.

3. Fill out all forms completely and accurately. It sometimes helps to photocopy the forms first so you can use one as a "practice sheet."

4. Notify all people that you have listed on the forms that they will be receiving requests for written reports, and notify physician and school

offices that records will be requested. Reiterate the importance of providing accurate information.

5. About three weeks after submitting the forms to Social Security, contact them to follow up on what records and reports they have received and which ones are missing.

6. Follow up on missing reports and provide any additional information the examiner may need.

Unfortunately, the SSI process can be a tedious one. Many parents feel like the disability examiners are there to disallow any application, but don't let this get in your way. The odds are high you will be rejected on the first try unless your child is profoundly autistic or has other medical conditions; this shouldn't stop you from attempting to get her disability allowed. If you are rejected, you can appeal and it is quite common for disallowed cases to be allowed in review. If you are approved on appeal, your child's benefits will be back-dated to the date that the claim was disallowed, which can be a sizeable sum of money that will help offset the expenses you have incurred since then.

Medical Coverage

There are few things more important than medical coverage, particularly when a family member has a disorder such as autism. Unfortunately, most private insurances have an exclusion for autism and will not cover anything that is in any way related to the diagnosis of an autism spectrum disorder. However, there are things you can do to increase your coverage amounts:

- When you call for a doctor's appointment for your child, tell the receptionist what the physician is seeing your child for. If it is a sore throat, for example, tell them that at the time of making the appointment.

- If your physician's office has a sign-in form, sign your child's name and write down the complaint that you are in for, even if there is not a place on the form for that information.

- When the nurse comes into the examination room and asks the reason for the visit, if it is not related to autism, there is no reason to state that your child has autism. Unless it is a physician you have not seen before, your doctor knows your child has autism.

- When the doctor sees your child, be certain to stress at the beginning of the visit that your reason for being there is not his autism.

- Upon leaving the office, you will most likely be presented with a copy of the insurance slip. Check the section for diagnosis and be sure autism is not circled or written in—it is an irrelevant diagnosis if the problem was a sore throat or another unrelated condition.

None of this is dishonest. Most physicians and their staff include all the diagnoses a person has on an insurance form, without realizing that only the diagnosis pertinent to the visit should be documented. Strep throat or a checkup has nothing to do with autism, and your insurance should cover it just as it would with any other family member.

DID YOU KNOW?

The disabled adult children's benefits, through Social Security, are available to adult children disabled prior to age twenty-two and whose parents are no longer able to provide for them due to retirement, disability, or death. These can help offset expenses later in life.

This is one of the reasons SSI is so important. With SSI comes Medicaid, which is a state-funded health insurance that does not exclude autism-related visits from its coverage. Even if your SSI drops to a level that seems hardly worth having, you will still have the Medicaid and it will ease your financial burden. If you have no other medical coverage for autism, keeping Medicaid is high on your list of priorities. You will still have to qualify for Medicaid by meeting certain income requirements, but it should be a consideration in your financial planning.

Creative Financial Assistance

The United States is the only "first-world" country that pays for a person's medical needs in an institution but that does not assist in keeping a family member at home. It is not sound social planning, and it certainly is poor financial planning as it costs much less to have people cared for at home. It costs 70 percent less to use respite care instead of institutional living. Parents can take a proactive approach and find many ways to secure financial assistance as they deal with the cost of autism.

Different States, Different Help

Throughout the United States, different assistance programs and benefits are available. Each of these depends on the state in which you live. Although most assistance does come from a federally funded program, it is administrated on state levels, and each of the fifty states has its own regulations.

Some states have programs known as Family Support Funds. The Developmental Disability Center (DDC) in each state manages these funds. Qualifying for these funds is easy, and parents are usually taken on their word about a child's disability. Payments can be as low as $500 a year and as high as $500 a month. The only requirement is that the funds distributed to each family must be used for the benefit of the child with the disability. Call the local DDC and ask about funds of this nature. If you are unable to find any resources, ask your support group, who will likely know what is available.

A BETTER PARENTING PRACTICE

If you are on the lower end of the income scale, you still have a potential tax benefit. The Earned Income Credit (EIC) may give you a refund that is actually larger than the taxes you pay! This program was put in place to assist what the government terms the "working poor" and can help single-parent families as well as families who are struggling to get by each month.

Additionally, when you file your state income tax, find out if there is another deduction for the disability that your child has. Some states will allow two deductions for a child with autism or another disability. Others do not. Check into your state's laws to be sure you are receiving every tax benefit possible.

A True Tax Incentive

Every family that pays taxes has a way to receive a lump-sum "benefit" annually. But did you know that taxes also provide a way to save money? Deductions are available to most families and although filing with listed deductions is more complex, it can make a big difference. Itemizing deductions means using the actual expenses you have incurred throughout the previous year instead of the government's estimated standard deduction. Do you know that you can deduct just about anything that is necessary to treat the medical condition of any member of your family? Here are some ideas, but consult a tax professional to be sure about the specifics of deductions.

- Health insurance costs paid by you for medical, dental, and prescription coverage
- Physician visits that you pay for (not covered by insurance)
- Co-payments that are required for medical services
- Medical equipment that is necessary and prescribed (and not covered by insurance) by any member of your family
- Deductibles on your health insurance that you are financially responsible for

- Contact lenses and glasses as well as the supplies that are needed to care for them
- Prescribed birth control
- Insulin
- Transportation to medical care or therapy

And remember, if you can reduce the amount you owe in federal taxes, you will also be reducing your state income tax. Speak with a tax expert or accountant to find the best options for your family.

Respite Care

By the time some parents hear about respite care, they are already exhausted and burned out. No one can do it all, but parents of children with autism seem compelled to attempt it, and they do quite well. The autism community has many remarkable parents who have been tested by fire and come out stronger for it. But everyone needs a break from autism—that includes you!

A Service for the Whole Family

Respite care is for both the caregiver (you) and the person with a disability (your child) to have a break from the daily routine of being together. It is beneficial for the child, and it is essential for the parent. A special-needs child is not an independent element in your household. Everyone in the family is affected by his needs, and you will spend a lifetime to accomplish this adjustment. This is why respite care is a family service; it is there to assist the entire family as they care for a disabled child at home.

DID YOU KNOW?

Respite care is beneficial for your child as well as for yourself. Having other people take charge at times will put some variety in your child's life and teach her that she can, and should, communicate with others. Work with the respite caregiver so he understands the communication system your child uses.

If your child is newly diagnosed, you may not be able to even consider leaving him with another individual. This is a normal reaction and you shouldn't do anything you are uncomfortable with. There will be a time that you will be open to the idea, but in the meantime, just keep it in the back of your mind as an option.

Finding a Respite Care Worker

When you discuss respite care options, have a list of questions ready. Are you interested in short-term or long-term respite? Is the care provided in your home or in another place? What kind of costs are involved and what type of assistance is available? And where do you find care? You will want to know how a service selects respite care workers, what kind of training they have, and if they are experienced in first aid and CPR. Health and Human Services or the social workers you work with can guide you in finding the respite care that is appropriate for your family. Ask if you can meet the respite care worker who will be assigned to your child before your child meets him or her. It is also important, because of the routine that people with autism have, to know if the same care worker will be available each time for your child. It could be once a month or twice a month that you get to take advantage of respite care. You will be provided services based on your family's needs and the availability of respite care workers in your area.

As your child matures into adulthood, respite care can be used to assist in the building of skills. Considering that most adults with autism do live in a group home environment, the experience of respite care can help families with the transition when that time arrives. There are many services and resources available; it is just a matter of discovering them. You will likely be able to find something that you are comfortable with.

Support for Parents

It is not uncommon for parents to feel a sense of isolation when they learn their child has autism. After some time passes you will feel less isolated, and you will learn that autism is not the most devastating of disabilities. Isolation is not something you have to learn to live with. There are many forms of support available to you that are worth taking advantage of.

A BETTER PARENTING PRACTICE

If you need to find a physician or dentist, ask at your support group meeting. The people there will have the information that you need and will be able to give you their opinion of the care that they received. Recommendations from people you know, especially people who may share concerns similar to yours, are a great way to find the services you need to provide for your child.

Looking for support does not make a person weak. Rather, it creates a foundation of stability and knowledge that imparts security and confidence. A support group, just by its presence, will remind you that you aren't alone in your daily struggles. You will learn that they too worry about what will happen when their child is an adult—they have the same fears and concerns that you have. They will reassure you that you did nothing to cause this to happen to your child and will rejoice with your victories and cry with your disappointments.

Finding the Right Support Group

Just as every treatment isn't right for your child, not every support group will be right for you. Some support groups are founded on a belief in a certain treatment. If you do not feel comfortable with a particular treatment that is the foundation for a support group, it wouldn't be a good fit for you. They provide specialized support for those who follow a certain theory, and that is fine, but don't ever join a group with the idea that you can change its focus. That isn't fair to them or you.

What Are the Differences?

Different areas have different kinds of support groups. There are large ones and small ones, groups that meet weekly and some that meet monthly, ones with and without babysitting provided, and others that serve particular age groups.

If you have never been part of a support group, consider joining one that is general in its nature and approach. The main emphasis should be on coping with autism and its behaviors. This type of group may be directed to families of children with any disorder.

General Disabilities or ASD-Specific?

One of the first decisions to make in selecting the right support group for you is whether you want a group for parents of children with any disability or one that is for parents of autistic children only. There are good things about either type of group. Some of this may depend on the community in which you live—it may be hard to find very specific support groups near smaller towns.

DID YOU KNOW?

One rule that is absolutely followed in any support group is not to criticize other people for their decisions about treatment and therapy for autism. Keep your comments and opinions positive and helpful. Every person is entitled to his or her opinion and should be treated with respect.

Groups that support families who have children with various disabilities bring a great deal of variety into a discussion and the group dynamics. If you have never been to a support meeting, you may think you would have little in common with a mother holding a baby that depends on a feeding tube. You will be surprised at how much you do have in common once you begin to talk and learn about each other's daily lives. Parents of deaf children will have a lot of advice about handling simple communication issues; even though their children may have receptive speech, they know what a lack of expressive speech means to a family.

One of the most significant benefits of a group that supports various disabilities is the way it will dispel the isolation. When you see other parents dealing with issues far different from yours, yet just as (if not more so) disabling, and surviving, you will no longer feel as alone. Meeting people who deal with children who are physically and/or mentally challenged puts life into perspective and things become more manageable.

Groups that support only parents of children with autism have some great benefits as well. Parents who deal with autism on a daily basis are not going to so much as lift an eyebrow if your child empties out your purse and lines up everything that was in it on the floor. That is "standard operating procedure" to those parents. They know what a meltdown is and won't stare at you when your child demonstrates one right in the middle of the parking lot as you are leaving. They understand elopement and how fearful it is. And they won't assume your child will talk to them; they will understand the limitations of a nonverbal child.

Support on the Internet

The Internet may be one of the greatest inventions of the twentieth century. Never before in human history can so many people be instantly in contact with any part of the world at any time of the day or night. The cost of the equipment is reasonable in price and few areas are inaccessible. The wealth of information you can find online is staggering. If you need it, or want it, or have to understand it, you can find it online.

An autism community on the Internet is much like any other community. It has information, people, discussions, planned meetings (chats), shopping, and many personal opinions from the community population. You can find resources that can be trusted; just remember to pay attention to the source of the information.

One of the major advantages to autism communities on the Internet is the accessibility factor. They are open twenty-four hours a day, seven days a week. They are good for middle-of-the-night ranting and raving, and they are wonderful for people who live in isolated areas. If you have a work schedule that prohibits your attending a real-life support group, the Internet is your next best bet. And if you have a real-life support group, the knowledge you gain on the Internet can enhance your group meetings.

Appendix B (see p. 203) has sources on the Internet that are valuable for anyone close to a child with autism. If you are new to the world of cyberspace, find a good book on how to get around on the web to find the resources you are searching for. Check out various communities and discover the volume of information that can help you as you learn about autism.

Glossary

activities of daily living (ADL)
The activities that each person engages in daily for personal care and hygiene. Dressing and bathing are examples.

American Sign Language (ASL)
The primary sign language used in the United States. It was developed for people with deafness and is often conceptually based.

applied behavioral analysis (ABA)
A therapy method that uses positive reinforcement to encourage appropriate behaviors to help an individual with autism function in society. Also called the Lovaas method, after Dr. Ivar Lovaas.

Area Education Agency (AEA)
Provides support services (educational consultation, mental health, social work, nursing, speech and language, etc.) to local education agencies.

Asperger's syndrome (AS)
A disorder on the autism spectrum characterized by normal speech and social difficulties. Diagnosis may not occur until the child is older.

Aspie
A person with Asperger's syndrome.

attention deficit hyperactivity disorder (ADHD)
A developmental disorder in which children can have symptoms of inattention and get distracted easily and/or have hyperactivity and impulsivity.

auditory processing disorder (APD)
A disorder in which language is heard correctly but not understood or not processed correctly by the brain.

augmentative and alternative communication (AAC) A communication aid to assist people with limited or no verbal ability. A communication board is the most commonly used tool.

autie
A person with autism.

autism
A neurological disorder characterized by communication difficulties (expressive and receptive), sensory problems, and socialization issues. Usually appears between sixteen months and two years of age.

Autism Society of America (ASA)
One of the leading autism organizations in the United States.

autism spectrum disorders (ASD)
A collection of disorders characterized by symptoms such as impaired verbal ability and social dysfunction.

beneficiary
The recipient of a trust fund, life insurance policy, or other assets and funds that have been designated to go to that person.

boardmaker
A device that resembles a notebook or board game created to help nonverbal people communicate.

central auditory processing disorder (CAPD)
A disorder that interferes with the combination of abilities that enables a person to obtain meaning from language.

Diagnostic and Statistical Manual of Mental Disorders, 4th edition (DSM-IV)
A publication used to diagnose autism spectrum disorders. The fourth edition is the most current version of this publication.

echolalia
The verbal repetition of words without using those words for any communication or meaning.

elopement
The tendency of a child with autism to "escape" his or her environment and wander off, usually with no particular direction in mind.

encopresis
A bowel disorder where very hard stool forms in the rectum and liquid stool leaks out from above. Causes bowel leakage.

Exact Sign Language
A form of sign language (using much of American Sign Language) that has a sign for each word. Also known as "Exact English."

expressive speech
The ability to utilize spoken language to convey ideas, thoughts, and feelings.

facilitated communication
A controversial method of communication that uses the aid of another person for physical and emotional support.

flapping
The movement of the hand and forearm by a child or adult with autism that mimics a wave but occurs due to overstimulation, either physically or emotionally.

Free Appropriate Public Education (FAPE)
Programs for education that are individualized, meeting a student's needs and providing an education that progresses and is satisfactory.

gluten-free, casein-free diet (GFCF)
A diet used by many parents of children on the autism spectrum. The diet excludes all gluten and casein products.

high-functioning autism (HFA)
A form of autism that is much less disabling as an individual has verbal ability and varying degrees of social understanding. IQ will be measured at seventy or above.

imaginative play
The ability to play with objects using imagination. For example, toy cars, people, and houses can be a town in which an entire scenario is played out.

inclusive

A term used interchangeably with mainstreaming. Refers to a child with a disability having access to the same classroom as if he or she were not disabled.

Individual Education Plan (IEP)

An official plan, written on a yearly basis, that is developed at a meeting with parents, teachers, therapists, and other experts involved in a disabled child's education.

Individuals with Disabilities Education Act (IDEA)

A United States congressional act that dictates all the rights children with disabilities have in order to receive full educational benefits from public schools.

InLv

Independent living (support group); an abbreviation used to indicate a person with autism is functioning at a high enough level to live alone with minimal supervision, such as a social worker checking in daily.

IQ (intelligence quotient)

The number that is considered a standard for measuring a person's intelligence and capacity for understanding.

least restrictive environment (LRE)

An educational term that refers to the classroom or environment a student attends daily that provides the least amount of restriction to ensure safety and the most of social and educational interaction.

licensed clinical social worker (LCSW)

A mental health professional licensed by each state to help individuals and families.

low-functioning autism (LFA)
A more severe form of autism with IQ measuring at below seventy.

meltdown
The total loss of behavioral control by a person with autism.

mental retardation (MR)
Mentally retarded (IQ less than seventy).

multidisciplinary team (MDT)
Teacher, SLP (speech/language pathologist), occupational therapist, psychologist, and parents! Used in reference to the group of individuals who are a part of development and implementation of an IEP.

neuro-immune dysfunction syndrome (NIDS)
The possible connection between neuro-immune and/or auto-immune dysfunction and conditions such as autism, ADD, Alzheimer's, ALS, CFS/CFIDS, MS, and other immune-mediated diseases.

neuro-typical (NT)
A term used for children without autism who are "normal" by definition of society.

No Child Left Behind (NCLB)
An education reform act designed to improve student achievement. All states, school districts, and schools that accept Title I federal grants are subject to NCLB policy.

not otherwise defined (NOD)
Often appears with a diagnosis by a psychologist. This is a term that is used when a disorder is present but it does not fall into a specific definition within the diagnostic manuals.

not otherwise specified (NOS)
Used as a footnote on a diagnosis when the disorder is vague in many ways (usually seen as PDD-NOS). It is considered a "catch-all" diagnosis and is often not accepted as a valid diagnosis by insurance companies.

Obsessive-Compulsive disorder (OCD)
This is a disorder in which a person is obsessed with unwanted thoughts and feels the need to act out compulsive behaviors.

occupational therapist or occupational therapy (OT)
A therapist that works with improving fine motor skills as well as developing solutions for practical day-to-day living as deficits are accommodated.

parallel play
Playing beside another child, but playing independently and not interacting with that child.

physical therapist or physical therapy (PT)
A therapist or therapy that works to increase the functionality of gross motor skills.

picture exchange communication system (PECS/PCS)
A communication tool that uses photographs and/or drawings to replace words for language.

Prader-Willi syndrome
A disorder on the autism spectrum. PWS is a complex genetic disorder that typically causes low muscle tone, short stature, incomplete sexual development, cognitive disabilities, problem behaviors, and a chronic feeling of hunger that can lead to excessive eating and life-threatening obesity.

receptive speech

Hearing spoken language from another person and deciphering it into a meaningful mental picture or thought pattern, which is understood and then used by the recipient.

Rett syndrome (RS)

A disorder on the autism spectrum. Rett syndrome is a genetic neurological disorder seen almost exclusively in females and found in a variety of racial and ethnic groups worldwide. It is characterized by apparently normal or near normal development until six to eighteen months of life. A period of temporary stagnation or regression follows, during which the child loses communication skills and purposeful use of the hands.

savant

A person with autism who has unusual and brilliant intelligence. Appears in approximately 10 percent of people with autism.

selective serotonin reuptake inhibitor (SSRI)

A medication used for depression, anxiety, and the control of obsessive-compulsive behaviors, including Prozac, Zoloft, Paxil, and Luvox.

self-contained

In reference to special education, it refers to schools or classrooms containing only a special-needs population.

sensory overload

The reaction a child with autism has when more senses are being stimulated than he or she has the ability to process.

service animal
An animal that is trained to work with and meet the needs of a disabled person.

splinter skill
This is a highly refined skill accomplished by a child or adult with autism. Other skills may be below typical age level but one or two skills, such as music or computer programming, may be far above average.

stuffing
A characteristic of autism where the child overfills his mouth with food. The biggest hazard associated with stuffing is the risk of choking.

theory of mind
A human characteristic that acknowledges that each person has a mind and one individual may not be aware of the other person's thoughts. Communication bridges that gap.

therapy animal
An animal that is used to calm people who are either ill or disabled. The animal's job is to deliver unconditional love.

tic
A brief, repetitive, purposeless, nonrhythmic, involuntary movement or sound. Tics that produce movement are called "motor tics," while tics that produce sound are called "vocal tics" or "phonic tics." Tics tend to occur in bursts or "bouts."

Tourette's syndrome (TS)
Also known as Tourette syndrome or Tourette's disorder, this is a fairly common childhood-onset condition that may be

associated with features of many other conditions. This syndrome is characterized by tics.

Treatment and Education of Autistic and Related Communication Handicapped Children (TEACCH)

A method of teaching children with communication deficits that encourages communication with picture boards or other assistive devices.

Williams syndrome

A disorder on the autism spectrum. Williams syndrome is typically characterized by elfin face, dental problems, characteristic stenotic cardiovascular problems (narrowing of the blood vessels) and hypercalcemia (excessive calcium in the blood). People afflicted with Williams syndrome also have a characteristic tendency to approach strangers indiscriminately.

Appendix B

Additional Resources

The American Academy of Child and Adolescent Psychiatry
3615 Wisconsin Avenue, N.W.
Washington, DC 20016-3007
(202) 966-7300
Fax (202) 966-2891
www.aacap.org
The American Academy of Child and Adolescent Psychiatry provides important information as a public service to assist parents and families in their most important roles.

Autism Options
3435 Camino Del Rio South
Suite 107
San Diego, CA 92108
(619) 280-8585
www.autism-options.com
Autism Options offers families with children with autism ways to improve attention, motivation, behavior, and motor skills using sensory techniques.

About.com: Autism
http: //autism.about.com
The Autism site at About.com is one of the most comprehensive websites dealing with Autism and PPD. It has informa-

tion, links to resources, forum communities, and chat rooms, free to all.

Autism Research Institute

4182 Adams Avenue

San Diego, CA 92116

(866) 366-3361

Fax (619) 563-6840

www.autism.com

The Autism Research Institute (ARI), a nonprofit organization, was established in 1967. ARI is primarily devoted to conducting research, and to disseminating the results of research, on the causes of autism and on methods of preventing, diagnosing, and treating autism and other severe behavioral disorders of childhood. They provide information based on research to parents and professionals throughout the world.

Autism Society of America

7910 Woodmont Avenue, Suite 300

Bethesda, MD 20814-3067

(301) 657-0881 or (800) 3AUTISM

www.autism-society.org

ASA has more than 200 chapters in nearly every state reaching out to individuals with autism and their families with information, support, and encouragement.

Autism Speaks

5455 Wilshire Boulevard, Suite 715

Los Angeles, CA 90036

(323) 549-0500

Fax (323) 549-0547

www.autismspeaks.org

Autism Speaks is an organization of parents, physicians, and researchers dedicated to promoting and funding research with direct clinical implications for treatment and a cure for autism.

The BHARE Foundation

523 Newberry

Elk Grove, IL 60007

(847) 352-7678

bharefoundation@sbcglobal.net

www.bhare.org

The Brenen Hornstein Autism Research & Education (BHARE) Foundation's top priority is to fund research that will lead to a cure for autism. Good summaries for parents are available along with information regarding project funding.

Center for the Study of Autism

P.O. Box 4538

Salem, OR 97302

www.autism.org

The Center for the Study of Autism (CSA) is located in the Salem/Portland, Oregon area. The center provides information about autism to parents and professionals, and conducts research on the efficacy of various therapeutic interventions.

Children's Rights Council

8181 Professional Place, Suite 240

Landover, MD 20785

(301) 459-1220

info@crckids.org

www.crckids.org

The Children's Rights Council (CRC) is a national nonprofit organization that works to assure children meaningful and continuing contact with both their parents and extended family regardless of the parents' marital status.

Families for Early Autism Treatment, Inc. (FEAT)

P.O. Box 255722

Sacramento, CA 95865-5722

www.feat.org

Families for Early Autism Treatment (FEAT) is a California-based organization with chapters in several states. Among other things, FEAT publishes one of the most comprehensive, informative, and activist newsletters in the autism community.

Federation of State Medical Boards of the United States Inc.

P.O. Box 619850

Dallas, TX 75261-9850

(817) 868-4000 • Fax (817) 868-4099

www.fsmb.org

The Federation of State Medical Boards (FSMB) website allows you to research if there have been any serious disciplinary actions or professional peer reviews against a physician you are considering for your child.

For Parents Only.com

www.forparentsonly.com

For Parents Only.com is a specialized search engine connecting parents and information.

Free Appropriate Public Education (FAPE)

www.fapeonline.org

The Free Appropriate Public Education (FAPE) site is intended to be a beginning point for research by parents, educators, state and federal staff members, and other interested parties into a wide range of issues involving disabilities and disability law.

From Emotions to Advocacy (FETA)

www.fetaweb.com

From Emotions to Advocacy, the Special Education Survival Guide by Pam and Pete Wright, is an excellent resource for special education information. Fetaweb.com is the companion website to Wrightslaw.com.

International Society for Augmentative and Alternative Communication (ISAAC)

49 The Donway West, Suite 308

Toronto, ON M3C 3M9 Canada

(416) 385-0351 • Fax (416) 385-0352

www.isaac-online.org

The International Society for Augmentative and Alternative Communication (ISAAC) is an organization devoted to advancing the field of augmentative and alternative communication (AAC). The Mission of ISAAC is to promote the best communication for people with complex communication needs.

KeepKidsHealthy.com

www.keepkidshealthy.com

Keep Kids Healthy is an excellent pediatric medicine website.

Lovaas Institute

11500 West Olympic Boulevard, Suite 318

Los Angeles, CA 90064

(310) 914-5433 • Fax (310) 914-5463

www.lovaas.com

info@lovaas.com

The Lovaas Institute is a research-based program that specializes in teaching children with autism, pervasive developmental disorders, and related developmental disabilities. The program provides services nationwide.

The Medicine Program

P.O. Box 515

Doniphan, MO 63935-0515

(573) 996-7300

www.themedicineprogram.com

The Medicine Program may be able to help you with medication expenses. This organization was established by volunteers dedicated to alleviating the plight of an ever-increasing number of patients who cannot afford their prescription medication.

The National Autistic Society

393 City Road

London, EC1V 1NG, United Kingdom

44 (0)20 7833 2299 • Fax +44 (0)20 7833 9666

www.nas.org.uk

nas@nas.org.uk

The National Autistic Society (NAS) is the United Kingdom's foremost organization for people with autism and those who care for them, spearheading national and international initiatives and providing a strong voice for autism. The NAS works in many areas to help people with autism live their lives with as much independence as possible.

National Dissemination Center for Children with Disabilities (NICHCY)

P.O. Box 1492

Washington, DC 20013

(800) 695-0285 • Fax: (202) 884-8441

www.nichcy.org

nichy@aed.org

The National Information Center for Children and Youth with Disabilities (NICHCY) provides information on disabilities and disability-related issues. This organization is dedicated to providing information to parents and caregivers of children with disabilities, including autism/PDD.

National Organization of Social Security Claimants' Representatives (NOSSCR)

560 Sylvan Avenue
Englewood Cliffs, NJ 07632
(201) 567-4228 • Fax: (201) 567-1542
(800) 431-2804 (Lawyer Referral Service)
www.nosscr.org
NOSSCRatt.net

The National Organization of Social Security Claimants' Representatives (NOSSCR) has a referral service for claimants looking for a private attorney and Social Security benefit information and representation. They also have a caller hotline number for SSI children's benefits. The referral is free; the attorney will charge for the representation if the claim is successful.

National Network for Immunization Information

301 University Blvd.
Galveston, TX 77555-0350
(409) 772-0199 • Fax: (409) 772-5208
www.immunizationinfo.org

The National Network for Immunization Information works to dispel many of the myths and misinformation about vaccines by providing scientifically accurate and up-to-date information.

Neuro Immune Dysfunction Syndromes (NIDS) Research Institute

NIDS MEDICAL ADVISORY BOARD

(888) 540-4999

www.nids.net

The Neuro Immune Dysfunction Syndromes (NIDS) Research Institute is dedicated to increasing the public's awareness of the possible connection between neuro-immune and/or auto-immune dysfunction and conditions such as autism, ADD, Alzheimer's, ALS, CFS/CFIDS, MS, and other immune-mediated diseases. If your family has an autoimmune illness situation as well as autism, you will want to check this out.

No Child Left Behind (NCLB)

U.S. Department of Education

400 Maryland Avenue, SW, 7E-247

Washington, DC 20202

(800) 872-5327 • Fax: (202) 401-0689

www.ed.gov

The No Child Left Behind website includes a simple overview of the legislation, key dates to remember, frequently asked questions, information about what is happening in states across the country, and more importantly, where you can go to learn more and become involved. The goal of No Child Left Behind is to create the best educational opportunities for our nation's children and to ensure that they have every opportunity to succeed.

Parenting Special Needs

http://specialchildren.about.com

The Special Children site at About.com contains just about everything you need to know about raising children with special needs.

Patient Centered Guides' Autism Center

O'Reilly Customer Service

1005 Gravenstein Highway North

Sebastopol, CA 95472

(800) 998-9938 or (800) 889-8969 • Fax: (707) 829-0104

www.patientcenters.com/autism

The Patient Centered Guides' Autism Center is for families of those living with a pervasive developmental disorder. Much of the material here is for those in the middle of the autistic spectrum, particularly those with a diagnosis of PDD-NOS or Atypical PDD or those still trying to find a correct diagnosis. You can find articles and resources about PDDs, diagnosis, drug treatments, therapies, supplements, education, insurance, family life, other coping topics, and resources.

Social Security Administration

www.ssa.gov

The Social Security Administration website

Wrightslaw.com

www.wrightslaw.com

Wrightslaw.com is one of the most thorough websites regarding autism and special education. Parents, advocates, educators, and attorneys come to this site for accurate, up-to-date information about special-education law and advocacy for children with disabilities.

INDEX

when your
child has ...